Effective Learning Environments: Creating a Successful Strategy for Your Organization

Reza Sisakhti

American Society for Training & Development

Effective Learning Environments

Creating a Successful Strategy for Your Organization

Reza Sisakhti

ASTD

Ordering information: Books published by the American Society for Training & Development can be ordered by calling 800.628.2783 or 703.683.8100.

Library of Congress Catalog Card Number: 98-73229
ISBN: 1-56286-092-5

To my wife, Farah, for her love and enthusiastic support of all my endeavors, including the writing of this book.

Contents

Acknowledgments

The concept of effective learning environments is the product of my cumulative experiences as a student and practitioner in the field of human performance improvement. The processes and concepts described in this book are the products of practical day-to-day work helping people develop skills and knowledge that improve their performance and that meet the business objectives of their organizations. Although I cannot possibly list them all here, I would like to thank everyone who contributed to this work.

My special thanks go to those who taught me, including my students at Boston University who patiently listened to my conceptualization of effective learning environments and constructively challenged me to crystallize the concept, articulate its added value, and clarify the process for creating it.

I would like to thank my clients who challenged me to solve their learning and development problems over the years. They invited me into their organizations and gave me a chance to explore their problems, learn about their situations, and experiment with innovative solutions.

Many colleagues at Digital Equipment Corporation were instrumental in making this book happen. My first thanks go to Janet Costales, for her inspiration, as well as the great support she extended while I was writing this book. Darlene Burton also deserves special thanks. Over the years she provided me with opportunities to solve tough learning issues in a complex and dynamic service organization. Special thanks go to my friend and colleague Rande Neukam for helping me to articulate the concept of effective learning environments more accurately and for putting into operation two components of the environment—mentoring and internships.

Finally, I am grateful to Deborah Smith who generously reviewed the first draft of the manuscript. Her superb editorial assistance was essential to getting this book done.

I would be remiss if I did not thank my son for his enthusiasm and his interest in seeing this book finished.

Preface

Contemporary organizations face a formidable challenge. They must help their workforces to develop and maintain a complex set of dynamic skills and knowledge if they are to gain and maintain a competitive advantage. A deficiency in the required skills or skill obsolescence can threaten an organization's ability to meet commitment and customer expectations, revenue and growth objectives, and employee satisfaction and loyalty metrics.

Conventional learning solutions (such as prepackaged instructional materials or instructor-led prescheduled training events) alone cannot help organizations meet this challenge. What can meet the challenge is an effective learning environment. An *effective learning environment* is a set of well-orchestrated opportunities for formal learning, for sharing information and experience, and for development. These opportunities are responsive to the ever-changing needs of an organization. An effective learning environment is not a "one-size-fits-all" solution; it offers a wide range of learning opportunities. It is not a "once-in-a-lifetime" opportunity; it is an ongoing feature of a work environment. Finally, it is not "cast in concrete"; it adapts quickly to business, work, and learner requirements.

This book introduces the concept of effective learning environments as a solution to the skill development and maintenance challenge faced by dynamic organizations. This book is designed to help you to

- develop an understanding of the challenge that organizations face in helping their workforces to develop a complex set of dynamic skills and in fighting skill obsolescence

- learn about the attributes of effective learning environments as a possible solution to meet the challenge in skill development

- develop an understanding of the business imperatives for creating effective learning environments
- learn about the components of effective learning environments (that is, formal learning opportunities, information- and experience-sharing opportunities, and development opportunities) and about the rationale, appropriate use, and requirements for successful implementation of each component
- develop skills in designing, developing, implementing, and orchestrating effective learning environments
- develop skills in evaluating the effectiveness and business impact of effective learning environments
- develop an understanding of the variables that help or hinder the creation of effective learning environments.

The ideas in this book are the product of my practical experiences in solving tough skill development problems in various organizations over the past two decades. I have shared the idea of creating effective learning environments with my colleagues and students in different organizations, industries, and countries. Their response has been overwhelmingly positive. Their enthusiasm has encouraged me to write this book, in the hope that it will serve as a useful learning opportunity for others in this inter-disciplinary field of human performance improvement and that it will be a small step in building an effective learning environment for us all.

Part 1
The Challenge and a Solution

The effective learning environment is a strategic tool for improving workplace performance. Effective learning environments are a solution to the challenge of skill development and maintenance faced by contemporary organizations.

Chapter 1 describes five variables that contribute to the complexity of this challenge and explains how the challenge threatens an organization's agility in accomplishing its objectives.

Chapter 2 defines the *effective learning environment* as a set of integrated opportunities—opportunities for formal learning, sharing information and experience, and development—opportunities that are responsive to business, work, and individual requirements.

Skill Development Challenge
Faced by Organizations

The Challenge

The skill development and maintenance challenge faced by organizations today is produced by the interaction of a number of factors: (1) skill complexity, (2) constant changes in required skills, (3) a lack of resident expertise, (4) a changing workforce, and (5) a lack of uniformity in skill deficiency. These factors are further compounded by their cumulative effect. Let's take a closer look at these factors.

Skill complexity

In today's workplace, both managers and individual contributors need a complex set of skills and knowledge to complete the work of their organization. The complexity is caused by three variables—the large number of required skills and knowledge domains; the diversity of the required skills and knowledge; and the need for integrating a large number of varied skills and knowledge areas. The following example illustrates the complexity factor.

Recently I completed a study of the skills needed by a group of computer service professionals to provide help desk support. These service professionals received telephone calls from end users experiencing a wide range of problems with their computer systems in a desktop-computing environment. Each caller expected a satisfactory resolution to the problem within a time period defined by contract, typically less than three hours after reporting the problem.

The service professionals were responsible for the following tasks:

• interacting with the customer to define the problem

- using their expertise and a support environment to solve the problem
- closing the call to the customer's satisfaction.

Their support environment consisted of a set of tools to simulate the customer's problem, a database of known problems and solutions, and other colleagues who had specialized knowledge in various computing domains and could consult with them to solve more complex problems. These professionals supported about 90 software products ranging from operating systems (for example, Macintosh, Windows 95, Windows NT) to personal computer (PC) networking systems (for example, TCP/IP), to popular applications (for example, Microsoft Office or Lotus Suite), to specialized applications (for example, Microsoft database, Intuit).

The study showed that the computer service professionals needed proficiency in no fewer than 184 discrete skills and knowledge areas to complete their work. These skills could be grouped into two broad categories: technical and professional. The technical category ran the entire gamut of skills from fundamentals of information technology, to advanced troubleshooting techniques, to different areas of specialization. The professional category included business and communication skills, tools skills, and context knowledge. Table 1.1 illustrates examples of the computer service professional's needed skills and knowledge in both technical and professional categories.

This example illustrates two variables that contribute to skill complexity: number and variety. Equally important is the integration variable. Professionals do not use their skills and knowledge in isolation. The study showed that a well-rounded service professional needs to integrate a large number of varied skills and knowledge areas into a holistic set in order to be able to solve customer problems effectively and efficiently. For example, strong grounding in the fundamentals of information technology (IT) provides them with a thorough understanding of computing environments and enables them to adapt more effectively to the customers' changing computing environments. They are able to move across environments and to learn about them more quickly. The specialized skills and knowledge give service professionals focus and enable them to respond effectively and efficiently to specific customer requests for help. Solid troubleshooting skills complement their technical expertise and make them

Table 1.1: Examples of skills needed by computer service professionals.

Technical Skills	Professional Skills
Information technology foundation skills • Broad knowledge of desktop computing • Knowledge of interoperability issues • Broad knowledge of major categories of PC applications (spreadsheets, word processing, project management) • Knowledge of computing technologies (for example, databases, networking) • Knowledge of operating systems (for example, Windows) **Troubleshooting skills** • Ability to interpret computer error messages • Ability to replicate customer problems for analysis • Ability to determine appropriate course of action **Specialized skills in one or more domains, such as** • Technology (for example, PC networking, databases) • Applications (for example, Lotus 1-2-3, Excel, and Microsoft Word)	**Business and communication skills** • Business skills • Customer relations skills • Account management skills • Project management skills • Communication skills • Team-building skills • Technical selling skills **Tools skills** • Productivity tools (for example, Microsoft Office) • Troubleshooting tools (for example, database of known problems and solutions) **Context Knowledge** • Customer knowledge • Organization knowledge (that is, knowledge of organization's products, services, strategic directions, organizational structure, and support systems) • Industry knowledge (awareness of both competition and partners)

valued service providers to customers with complex computing environments. Their professional skills and knowledge enable them to communicate well with their customers and colleagues and make them valuable members of a service delivery organization.

The complexity of this required skill set is not unique to the high-tech industry. Professionals in most contemporary organizations need a large set of varied yet well-integrated skills and knowledge areas to contribute effectively to the success of their organizations. For example, a study I recently completed to define the required skills and knowledge for human resource development professionals showed that instructional designers and course developers need to be proficient in 154 and 125 skill and knowledge areas, respectively.

The complexity of the required skill set poses major challenges to traditional skill development practices. Single-point-solution training events and unstructured on-the-job training—the hallmarks of a traditional training approach—are unlikely to work. The same variables that contribute to the complexity of a required skill set (that is, number, diversity, and need for skills integration) impose unique requirements on an organization's skill development and maintenance activities. A few weeks of classroom instruction per year are not sufficient to help the desktop service professionals described earlier to develop and maintain the large number of skills needed to complete their work. The diversity of the needed skills demands diversity in the methods used to facilitate skill acquisition and maintenance. The methods best used to develop professional skills are different from the methods best used to develop expertise in specialized areas. Some skill development efforts (for example, learning foundation skills) require a didactic approach (for example, a lecture on differences between relational and nonrelational databases), some require a hands-on approach (for example, honing solution definition skills), and some require a cognitive apprenticeship approach (for example, fine-tuning one's customer relations skills). The integration of required skills demands learning and development opportunities that are continuous rather than event driven. Professionals working to build their skills need to observe complex behaviors of master performers on the job, model their behaviors while being observed, and receive meaningful feedback as they successively approximate the desired behavior.

The challenge of skill complexity is due to the large number of required skills, the diversity of those skills, and the need to integrate a large number of these diverse skill and knowledge areas. Only multifaceted, continuous, systemic learning and development opportunities can meet the challenge.

Constant changes in required skills

Work settings are changing constantly and dramatically. A number of variables contribute to this continuous change, for example: (1) constantly changing customer needs, desires, and requirements; (2) a continuously evolving portfolio of product and service offerings; (3) continuously changing tools, processes, and practices; and (4) shifts and rapid changes in the general business environment. These changes individually or in combination cause skill deficiency at an unprecedented rate. As a result, employees need to upgrade their skill sets continuously to respond to the requirements imposed by an ever-changing work environment. Consider the earlier example of computer service professionals who support approximately 90 software products. On average, an upgraded version of the product is offered every six to nine months, and a new version (similar to the change from Microsoft Windows to Windows 95) is offered every nine to 18 months. Some upgrades are major product revisions that cause incompatibility problems with earlier versions of the same product and other related products. In addition, new products are frequently introduced, new tools and methodologies for troubleshooting and service delivery are offered, and new alliances and partnerships are announced, which impact the list of supported products. This constant change in required skills is compounded by the need to update those skills rapidly. Speed in fighting skill obsolescence in a rapidly changing environment is a crucial success factor. In many cases, the window of opportunity for developing a new skill is very small.

Lack of resident expertise

As organizations focus on their core competencies and establish new alliances and partnerships to provide complex products and services, they cannot assume that all expertise required to complete the work or to train employees will already reside within the organization. In the example of service professionals, the majority of the products on the supported product list were third-party products. Most software vendors (for example, Microsoft and Lotus) had service contracts with the service center to support their products.

Consequently, creating training solutions that rely primarily on access to internal subject matter expertise (for example, the engineers who design the products) may not be feasible. Building another dimension into an organization's alliance and partnership relations—a relationship that involves access to subject matter experts and facilities in the partner's organization—may be reasonable. This relationship can facilitate developing and offering meaningful learning opportunities. These opportunities may include sabbaticals, experience and information sharing, and technical seminars.

Changing workforce

The nature of employment has changed. These days, employees usually stay with a company for shorter periods of time than is traditional and circulate as contractors or consultants in a host of related industry settings.

This arrangement offers several benefits to organizations. It might reduce cost by creating a variable workforce. It provides rapid access to expertise that can take years to develop internally. It results in the infusion of new approaches to work, when temporary or new workers join an organization. A disadvantage is the loss of intellectual capital and continuity of support when employees leave their jobs.

The new employment reality has created unique challenges. Effective fast-start learning opportunities can help the temporary workforce learn about the new work context and begin making a contribution quickly. Opportunities should also be provided to tap into the expertise of the newcomers and to disseminate their knowledge throughout the organization.

Lack of uniformity in skill deficiency

The learning and development needs of each employee are unique. Different groups and individuals within a single group have unique skill development requirements depending on their experiences, prior knowledge, and particular ways of processing information.

The changing nature of the required skills and knowledge, coupled with a dynamic workforce, has made large-scale, uniform training programs less practical. Learning opportunities need to be more specific and more carefully aimed at the needs of the individual learner. To be meaningful, a training intervention of one size cannot fit all.

To accommodate diversity in skill deficiencies among employees, learning opportunities should be self-paced (versus group-based), available on demand (versus prescheduled), and available in a convenient location. Organizations should tap the skill strengths of employees and develop opportunities for coaching, mentoring, and cognitive apprenticeships to help learners overcome unique skill deficiencies.

Cumulative and Business Impact

Each of the factors discussed above contributes to the skill acquisition and maintenance challenge faced by contemporary organizations. The challenge becomes even more formidable when these factors interact, compounding each other's impact. Consider the computer service professionals, supporting about 90 software products that are being updated and replaced frequently. Using a complex set of tools, the service professionals interact on the phone to troubleshoot and solve all sorts of problems. The required skills and knowledge areas (a total of 184) are frequently changing and must be integrated. The expertise to troubleshoot and fix complex problems associated with many of the products resides in the engineering department of the product vendors, rather than in the organization. The makeup of their workforce is fluid: as new products are added to the list, service professionals with expertise in those products or computing domains are hired on a permanent or temporary basis. Each individual hired has unique skill deficiencies and development needs.

Obviously, this organization faces a formidable skill acquisition and maintenance challenge. The challenge is not only to acquire the needed skills, but also to fight skill obsolescence by constantly upgrading the skills.

The challenge of developing and maintaining a complex set of continuously changing skills manifests itself in many ways in an organization. Symptoms of this challenge include the following:

- Line managers struggle to find the right talent to staff projects and fulfill their commitments to their customers.
- Business managers are not able to keep up with customers' demands and as a result miss their growth objectives.
- Organizations are unable to replace skilled employees who are leaving their jobs to work for the competition.
- Overworked employees struggle to keep up with the demand for their expertise.

Failure to meet the challenge of developing new skills and conquering skill obsolescence can hurt the productivity of an organization and can threaten its ability to accomplish its business objectives. This challenge is not unique to high-tech industries. Continuous changes in customer needs; in the products and services provided by the organization; in tools; processes, and practices; and in the general business environment force many organizations to develop and maintain a set of complex and continuously changing skills in their employees. Clearly, the traditional isolated, prepackaged, prescheduled training events alone cannot help an organization meet this challenge, but an effective learning environment can.

Summary

Many contemporary organizations face a formidable skill development and maintenance challenge. Several factors contribute to this challenge:

- skill complexity
- constant changes in required skills
- a lack of resident expertise
- a changing workforce
- a lack of uniformity in skill deficiency.

Each factor individually contributes to the challenge of developing new skills and fighting skill obsolescence. The challenge becomes even more formidable when these factors interact and compound each other's impact.

2

Effective Learning Environments as a Solution

Conventional training and development solutions are not sufficient to meet the challenge in skill acquisition and maintenance faced by most contemporary organizations. An effective learning environment, however, can meet the challenge, because it matches the dimensions of each organization's skill development and maintenance challenge.

An effective learning environment surrounds learners with opportunities to learn new skills and continuously to upgrade existing skills. Because an organization's required skills are complex and change frequently, and because employees come and go, an effective learning environment offers multifaceted learning opportunities. The environment thus includes opportunities that range from structured courses to mentoring and from information-sharing sessions to sabbaticals.

An effective learning environment is integrated with the work itself. Learning opportunities are focused on the business and on what the learners need to know to contribute to it. Learning opportunities are designed to accommodate learners, whether beginner or expert, whatever their learning style. Because the learning opportunities are designed to teach learners just what they need to know, just the way they need to learn, the lessons are rigorous and demanding. Work does not stop and start, and the knowledge and skills required to perform the work change just as the workforce changes. To remain effective, a learning environment must be continuous.

How does an organization create an effective learning environment that has these attributes—an environment that is multifaceted, integrated with the work itself, focused on the business, accommodating to different learning styles, rigorous, demanding, and continuous? A systems approach helps to generate an effective learning environment that connects to other systems in an organization. Rapid prototyping allows an effective learning environment to change as quickly as the business itself changes.

What makes such an environment successful? Managers, learners, and their colleagues must support it and a robust reward structure should be in place to acknowledge that support.

This chapter examines the following topics in greater detail:

- attributes of an effective learning environment
- techniques for creating an effective learning environment
- commitment required for successful implementation of the environment.

The chapter ends with a case study of an organization that selected the effective learning environment as a solution to its skill development challenge.

Attributes of an Effective Learning Environment

Effective learning environments are (1) multifaceted, (2) continuous, (3) integrated with work, (4) accommodating to learners, (5) focused on business needs, and (6) rigorous and demanding.

Multifaceted learning opportunities

An effective learning environment consists of an integrated set of opportunities for formal learning, developing, and sharing information and experience. See figure 2.1 for an illustration of these learning opportunities, which are described in detail in the second part of this book.

An effective learning environment includes three general types of learning opportunity:

- *Formal learning.* These well-bounded learning opportunities, with clearly defined learning outcomes, are the most similar to the conventional learning interventions. They are designed to help learners gain knowledge or develop skills in a regulated, predefined

Figure 2.1: Components of an effective learning environment.

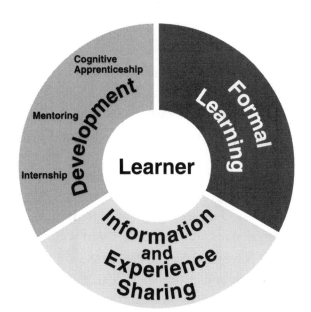

fashion. These learning opportunities can be self- or group-paced, instructor led or technology based. Examples are a computer-based learning module, an instructional video, a two-day workshop, a simulation, or a course in a local college.

- *Development opportunities.* These opportunities represent structured on-the-job learning with well-defined outcomes, durations, and required resources. Unlike traditional training interventions that are designed for an average or typical learner, development opportunities are created in response to the unique needs of each learner. Three types of development opportunities exist in an effective learning environment—mentoring, cognitive apprenticeships, and internships or sabbaticals.

- *Experience- and information-sharing opportunities.* These opportunities are intended to help employees reinforce existing skills and knowledge, stay current with new developments that impact their work, and revise skills and knowledge. Unlike formal learning opportunities, experience and information sharing tends to be spontaneous. These opportunities can be event driven (such as a brown-bag session on an upcoming model of a product) or continuous (such as an intranet-based notes conference for sharing workarounds for a new application).

Multifaceted learning opportunities meet the challenge of skill development and maintenance described in chapter 1. The following are factors that create this challenge and suggested solutions:

- *Skill complexity.* Employees need to develop and integrate a large number of diverse skills and knowledge areas. By providing access to a large number of formal learning opportunities, an organization can help employees satisfy their unique skill development needs. Structured on-the-job development opportunities allow learners to apply the acquired skills and integrate them with their existing skills.

- *Constant changes in required skills.* Provided with ample opportunities to share information and experience, learners can have access to the latest information and know-how and can constantly upgrade their skills and knowledge.

- *Lack of resident expertise.* Internships and sabbatical opportunities allow learners to go beyond the boundaries of an organization and benefit from expertise that does not reside in the organization.

- *Changing workforce.* Mentoring and opportunities to share information and experience enable more experienced employees to socialize new employees to the new organization and enable them to infuse knowledge into the organization.

- *Lack of uniformity in skill deficiency.* A wide variety of learning opportunities allows members of an organization to craft a tailored learning and development plan that is responsive to their skill development needs.

Continuous learning

Effective learning environments are continuous. The development of a complex set of dynamic skills is not a solitary, once-and-for-all-time event. It requires an ongoing effort, which comprises iterative opportunities for learning new skills and practicing and applying the newly learned skills in different settings to develop an appropriate degree of expertise. With structured development opportunities and continuous opportunities for sharing experience, learners can develop new complex skills and constantly upgrade them. Unlike traditional learning situations, an effective learning environment provides continuous learning, not only isolated events.

Integration with work

To be effective, development and maintenance of a complex set of dynamic skills should occur in the work setting. For example, how can a person effectively learn to sell a complex new product to a new market segment in a traditional classroom, using hypothetical examples and make-believe cases? By providing structured on-the-job development opportunities, such as cognitive apprenticeships and internships, an effective learning environment reduces the need for an artificial learning setting and integrates learning with work. Learners can observe master performers in the context of the work. Learners can model new behaviors while being observed by an expert and receive just-in-time feedback. Finally, they can perform the tasks in partnership with a master colleague to polish their skills and eventually perform the tasks independently.

Accommodation to learners

A lack of uniformity in the skill deficiency of employees, as well as a host of other individual differences among learners, makes one-size-fits-all learning events obsolete. Years of research in Aptitude Treatment Interaction (Snow, 1992; Snow and Swanson, 1992) show that differences in learners' personalities, cognitive abilities, and learning styles interact with variances in instructional methods and media to produce differences in outcome. Effective learning experiences adapt to learners' abilities, needs, past experience, and skill deficiencies. An effective learning environment provides learners with a variety of learning and development opportunities from which to choose and enables them to tailor a development plan based on idiosyncratic preferences and requirements.

For example, to help a project manager to develop skills in assessing and managing risks associated with a project, an effective learning environment provides the following learning opportunities:

- a computer-based learning module that describes project risk-assessment techniques in the context of a case

- a two-day course titled "Managing Risk on Projects," offered by Project Management Institute
- a half-day seminar, followed by a group discussion, on project risk-assessment techniques unique to the organization
- a meeting with a colleague who recently completed a high-risk project to discuss his or her experience and learn about the decision-making process that the colleague followed to determine and manage the risk factors in the project
- a mentoring opportunity providing insight from a colleague about sources of information on developing a risk-management plan
- access to the books *Practical Risk Assessment for Project Management* by Stephen Grey and *Project Risk Management: Processes, Techniques and Insights* by C.B. Chapman and Stephen Ward.

Depending on their preferences and skill development needs, employees can select, orchestrate, and utilize an appropriate number and combination of these options.

Focus on business needs

The most important factor in creating an effective learning environment is the business need of the organization. Business requirements dictate the structure, content, and resource allocation for effective learning environments. Effective learning environments help an organization to develop the needed *capability*—the required skills and knowledge to complete the work of the organization, and *capacity*—the number of people with required skills—to achieve its objectives. The organization's strategic business direction and evolving product and service portfolio determine the needed capability. For example, when an organization decides to offer a new service to its customers, the first task for architects of an effective learning environment is to determine what skills and knowledge areas are required to support the new service. They also must determine the needed capacity based on the sales forecast. The effective learning environment is thus a strategic business management tool that can help an organization acquire and maintain the needed capability and capacity to meet its business objectives.

Rigorous and demanding activities

Developing and maintaining a complex and dynamic set of skills is not an easy task. It requires a substantial amount of both time and energy on the part of the learners. Participants sometimes perceive conventional training as a benefit to reward high-performing employees. Some employees are accustomed to training events in which they can sit back, listen, and be entertained by the instructor. In contrast, employees in an effective learning environment are expected to participate actively. The following are examples of these learner activities:

- Assessing their skill development needs. Learning environments provide the learners with a variety of opportunities from which to choose. To take advantage of the learning opportunities, employees should define learners' skill development needs. Skill assessment is not done "once and for all time." Learners need to assess their skill development needs continuously.

- Selecting a complementary set of learning activities. To satisfy their skill development needs, employees must select a complementary set of learning and development options and orchestrate them in a personalized learning and development plan.

- Obtaining needed resources. Implementation of a personalized learning and development plan requires resources (budget, time, and support from colleagues). The learner must define and obtain needed resources. In the project management example cited earlier, the employee must obtain funding and time off work to attend the recommended risk management course, to take the computer-based learning modules, to read the books, or to participate in information- and experience-sharing opportunities. The employee must estimate the time commitment needed from experienced colleagues during the mentoring or experience-sharing sessions and obtain the required approvals.

- Making the necessary logistical arrangements. The employee may need to obtain required equipment, register for courses, arrange with the host organization to attend a sabbatical or internship, or define a mentoring agreement with an experienced colleague.

- Participating in learning activities. Most learning opportunities in an effective learning environment are rigorous and demanding. The employees need to be mindfully engaged during the learning activities. They also may need to do some preparatory study prior to attending the learning opportunity and be involved in post-learning activities.

- Monitoring their own progress and making necessary midcourse corrections. In an effective learning environment, employees are ultimately responsible for the appropriateness and effectiveness of their learning endeavors. They must constantly assess their progress toward accomplishing their skill development goals and make the necessary changes.

Techniques for Creating an Effective Learning Environment

To create an effective learning environment one needs to adopt a systems approach and use rapid prototyping techniques.

Systems approach

An effective learning environment is more than an array of learning and development activities. It is a holistic and comprehensive attempt to solve skill development problems faced by an organization. It is a subsystem within the larger system of an organization. The adoption of a systems approach (Gradous, 1989; Hayman, 1974) permits analysis of not only the internal workings of the learning environment itself but also the context in which it exists. A systems approach thus enables one to examine how harmoniously the components of an effective learning environment work together to solve the skill development and skill maintenance problems of an organization. This approach also encourages an understanding of the complex network of interactions between the learning environment and other subsystems within the organization, such as the work environment or the reward system. Using a systems approach ensures that

- each learning opportunity is well defined and has clearly articulated learning outcomes that are linked to an appropriate learning strategy

- appropriate links exist among the learning opportunities, so that they complement one another
- appropriate links exist between the learning environment and other subsystems within the organization (for example, employee rewards and compensation, recruitment, and hiring).

Rapid prototyping

The constantly changing nature of the required skills and the speed at which employees must develop them make conventional methods of creating learning and development options obsolete. Organizations can no longer afford the time required by linear training development models with long development cycles. The window of usefulness for learning interventions is narrowing quickly. Rapid prototyping techniques enable a learning environment to be agile enough to respond to sudden business changes. Instructional designers must continuously improve learning opportunities. They should base improvements on input and feedback from various constituencies, including employees as well as line and business managers. A rapid prototyping approach allows the environment to change with the speed required to develop and maintain a constantly changing skill set.

Required Commitment for a Successful Implementation

Successful implementation of an effective learning environment requires broad support from all involved constituencies (for example, employees, management, co-workers, and host organizations). A robust reward system encourages behavior in support of the learning environment.

Broad support

Employees must be committed to continuous improvement and must actively seek out and obtain learning opportunities. Effective learning environments acknowledge learner initiative and ownership as a cornerstone to successful implementation. Management must be committed to creating a hospitable learning climate, ensuring a match between learner and learning opportunity, providing resources and support, and enthusiastically endorsing each learner's initiative.

Colleague support and participation are crucially important to the success of the learning environment. The success of mentoring, cognitive apprenticeship, and information- and experience-sharing opportunities all depend, to a great extent, on the active participation and contribution of experienced colleagues and master performers.

Reward system

The successful design and implementation of an effective learning environment needs the cooperation and active participation of a number of individuals and groups within an organization. Many of these individuals and groups have traditionally abdicated their roles in developing and maintaining the required skill set to the training department and the instructors. The roles of these employees must change, as must the measurement of their performance. The organization should implement a robust reward system to encourage the required behavioral changes. An organization should

- reward business managers for considering skill development and skill maintenance as strategic operations within the organization and for actively participating in their successful implementation
- reward experienced colleagues and expert performers for actively participating in mentoring and cognitive apprenticeship opportunities. These activities help their colleagues to develop and maintain the required skill set
- reward colleagues who have unique areas of specialization or who obtain new experiences in the course of their work for sharing their knowledge, insight, and experiences with their colleagues formally and informally (for example, dialogues with colleagues, participation in online chat sessions, or written reports and white papers)
- recognize and reward employees for continuously learning new skills in support of the strategic direction of the organization.

To encourage active participation and support of learners, managers, and colleagues, organizations must put appropriate incentive programs in place. Examples of these programs include monetary rewards, recognition awards, positive performance reviews, and time off.

A Case Study

The following case study illustrates how a sales organization selected the effective learning environment as a solution to its skill development needs. A 200-person sales organization in a *Fortune* 500 medical equipment manufacturer was competing against well-entrenched competitors in a market segment. The sales organization was experiencing a number of problems caused by skill deficiency and obsolescence. Table 2.1 shows how deficient and outdated selling skills negatively affected the performance of the sales force.

The management team was intuitively aware of productivity problems associated with the deficient and obsolete skills of the sales force members. The sales training director commissioned a study to identify the selling skills and knowledge required for the sales force to compete effectively in the marketplace. Another goal of the study was to define the requirements for a training and development program that could successfully help the sales force to develop their required skills and knowledge. The study identified 129 skills and knowledge domains. These were grouped into 20 clusters, which were, in turn, grouped into the four categories shown in table 2.2. Table 2.3 is an example outlining the nine individual skills needed in a single cluster: designing solutions.

The study also revealed the following facts about the organization and the sales force:

Table 2.1: Impact of skill deficiency and skill obsolescence.

Skill deficiency and obsolescence led to...	Resulting in...
A shortage of qualified sales professionals	• Failure to meet current business metrics and commitments (for example, the sales force was not meeting its sales quota) • Failure to meet growth objectives (for example, the organization was not achieving the market share goals)
Increased pressure on qualified sales professionals to meet demands	• Reduction in innovation that compromised the competitive advantage of the organization • Burnout of qualified sales people
Too few opportunities for employees to learn from one another	• Loss of skilled employees to the competition
An inability to meet customer expectations	• Loss of customer confidence and loyalty

Table 2.2: Skill clusters needed by the sales force.

Categories	Skill Clusters
Background knowledge	• General business knowledge • General industry knowledge • Understanding of the health-care market • Understanding of the customers
Account management skills	• Strategic account planning skills • Account team management skills • Ability to get things done within the organization
General knowledge of the organization's technologies, products, and services	Knowledge of • Marketing strategy • Technologies, products, and services • Competitors • Financing strategies
Selling skills	Skills in • Breaking into new accounts • Analyzing the customer • Implementing competitive sales strategies and tactics • Building relationships • Consultative selling • Designing solutions • Proposing solutions • Financial selling • Delivering solutions

Table 2.3: Skills needed to design solutions.

- Ability to understand the needs of the customer and the kinds of solutions that can address those needs
- Ability to match the organization's solutions and technology to the customer's business problems and goals
- Ability to determine what is required to ensure compatibility with the customer's current operations
- Ability to assess what resources are required from the organization and from the customer to implement and manage the solution
- Ability to determine whether the organization has the resources to deliver and support the solution
- Ability to present the customer's needs and requirements to the organization
- Ability to define a solution that optimizes performance and costs
- Ability to put together an implementation plan, support plan, and customer training plan
- Ability to determine how to work with the customer's budgeting process

- A high turnover rate (more than 30 percent per year). This rate indicated a strong need for orienting new employees and integrating them into the organization.
- A diverse sale force. Each member of the sales force had unique skill development needs.
- Constant introduction of new products. The sales force needed constantly to upgrade their product knowledge.
- Selling of complementary medical equipment manufactured by other companies. The expertise to inform the sales force about these products did not reside in the organization.
- Overworked and thinly distributed sales force. The sales force could not take time off to attend training events due to other job commitments and travel restrictions.

The organization was a candidate to benefit from an effective learning environment. The learning environment could provide the sales force with opportunities to

- learn continuously about the products and their features, benefits, and shortcomings, as well as how they compare to competitors' products
- analyze customer problems and match them with the features of the product to formulate a solution
- tap into colleagues' experiences and learn from those who are exploring new ground
- observe and model the behavior of successful colleagues as they define a solution for a customer
- learn about decision-making and problem-solving processes used by a successful colleague
- learn about the cultural and political factors in a customer's organization and how they influence the customer's decision to evaluate a proposed solution
- learn to use needed tools and technology to define and propose solutions
- learn to predict customers' objections to a proposed solution and to modify the solution creatively.

The results of the study helped the management team realize that conventional training approaches alone were not capable of meeting the complexity of the skill development and skill maintenance challenges faced by their organization. The development of new skills and, more importantly, an ongoing upgrade of existing skills, constituted a complicated problem. To acquire and integrate a large number of varied skills that are constantly changing, the sales force needed more than a set of computer-based training modules distributed over the intranet, a few weeks of classroom instruction per year, or an unstructured mentoring engagement. These could all be elements of a solution, but the real solution needed to be comprehensive, multifaceted, and continuous. It needed to accommodate business requirements, the work environment, and learners' needs.

The management team agreed that fighting skill deficiency and obsolescence was a strategic business operation. They realized that an effective learning environment could provide the desired range of learning opportunities: formal learning; information and experience sharing; and mentoring, internship, and cognitive apprenticeship components. They understood that an effective learning environment could allow the organization to

- customize the learning opportunities for the sales force, because one size does not fit all
- target learning opportunities to specific employees and make them available conveniently to save learners' time—integrating training with work saves time and keeps employees on the job
- link learning opportunities with business requirements, in order to be responsive to continuous changes in the business strategy
- socialize newly hired employees to the organization and familiarize them with the work environment
- tap the skills and know-how of newly hired and experienced employees and disseminate that expertise throughout the organization.

The above example shows that deficient and outdated skills are a major threat to productivity, profitability, growth, customer loyalty, and employee satisfaction. Fighting skill deficiency and obsolescence is a strategic business operation that requires an innovative and effective solution. Conventional training methods and practices alone are not sufficient, but an effective learning environment can meet the challenge. Successful implementation of such an environment requires commitment from all levels of the organization, a new role for the training and development function, and involvement of management at all levels. Implementation of an effective learning environment is not a mere luxury: it is a business necessity.

Summary

An effective learning environment is built using a systems approach. This systems approach ensures the learning environment's effectiveness and links it to other systems in the organization. Rapid prototyping techniques allow the learning environment to adapt quickly to changes both in the business and in the workforce.

The learning environment that results has attributes not seen in traditional learning and development situations: multifaceted learning opportunities that are thoroughly integrated with the work and also are rigorous and demanding, a powerful focus on the business, and the ability to accommodate a wide range of learners. Also, this learning environment does not stop and start: it is continuous.

The success of an effective learning environment depends on broad support from the learners and their colleagues as well as from management, and that support must go beyond words. The organization needs a robust reward system because learners, managers, and colleagues must demonstrate new behaviors to make the learning environment successful.

Part 2
Components of an Effective Learning Environment

An effective learning environment consists of three major components: formal learning, the sharing of information and experience, and development opportunities. The first three chapters in this part define these components, provide criteria for their appropriate use, and state broad design guidelines. The last three chapters in this part focus on three types of development opportunities: mentoring, cognitive apprenticeships, and internships. For each development opportunity, these chapters will examine

- definitions and examples
- criteria for use
- requirements and dependencies
- practical design guidelines.

Although each component is described separately, it is important to keep in mind that in an effective learning environment learning opportunities flow into one another and complement each other. The added value of an effective learning environment is its holistic nature: an effective learning environment is more than the sum of its parts.

3

Formal Learning Opportunities

Formal learning opportunities are well-defined learning activities designed to help learners develop specific skills or gain knowledge in a specific area. Review the examples of formal learning opportunities listed in table 3.1.

Table 3.1: Examples of formal learning opportunities.

Formal Learning Opportunities	Designed to...
Computer-based simulation	Help sales professionals to match features of a new product or service with customers' needs
Electronic learning module accessible via intranet	Help a manager fill out an employee-appraisal form
Instructional video	Describe customer requirements in a new market segment
Half-day Interactive Broadcasting Television (IBTV) segment	Compare an organization's product with those of its major competitors
One-day simulation	Position a new product in a new market segment
Lecture by a subject matter expert followed by a facilitated discussion	Introduce a new business initiative
Series of courses offered by a college or a vendor on a specific topic	Help learners prepare for a certification or degree program
Set of audiotapes and workbooks	Develop skills in effective listening techniques
Two-day workshop	Familiarize service professionals with service-ability requirements of a new version of a product
Half-day orientation program	Help a new hire learn about the organization and employment benefits
Three-day lecture and lab	Help product design engineers develop skills in using a new design project management tool and process

These examples demonstrate that formal learning opportunities can be of various lengths, can use various formats and media, and can cover a wide range of content.

All of these formal learning opportunities can be divided into two broad categories—self-paced and group-based learning.

Self-Paced Learning Opportunities

Self-paced learning opportunities are independent learning situations in which a learner progresses through activities at his or her own pace. Examples are tutorials and text-based, video-based, and computer-based training. One of the advantages of self-paced learning opportunities is the flexibility of use that results when these opportunities are modularized, self-contained, and technology based. Learners can access them whenever and wherever they want without the need to schedule a classroom delivery event.

Self-paced learning opportunities are a significant component of the learning environment. The availability of a large number of self-paced learning modules enriches the learning environment. They provide tremendous flexibility to learners to access and utilize them just in time to develop a targeted skill or to gain specific knowledge. At Dell Computer Corporation, a large number of learning modules called "learning bites" are available through their intranet. At Digital Equipment Corporation, a collection of hundreds of courses and documents is available to employees through an intranet-based storage and distribution system called the Learning Utility. Learners can download the courses and learning modules at their desks and study them at their own convenience.

An organization may develop self-paced learning opportunities internally or acquire them from external vendors. For example, CBT Systems and GartnerLearning have hundreds of learning modules and courses available that can be accessed by employees of various organizations through contractual agreements, such as pay-per-view or flat rate arrangements.

Criteria for use

Self-paced learning opportunities are appropriate for the following situations:

- Desired learning outcomes are well defined. Some examples are when learners need to learn to follow a procedure (for example, order entry), use a new tool, or recall the features of a new product and match those features with potential customer needs and requirements. In both cases the learners need to develop specific skills and gain knowledge in a well-defined area.

- Content is well bounded. For example, a service professional might need to learn the procedure to close a customer call.

- Learning objectives can be accomplished independently by the learners through well-designed learning activities. The need for collaboration with another learner or subject matter expert in this situation is minimal. An example is learning to use a new contract administration tool to renew a customer's contract or to issue new contracts.

To use self-paced learning opportunities effectively, organizations must constantly review and evaluate existing and new learning modules, acquire new modules when needed, catalog modules carefully, and make them readily available to learners.

Group-Based Learning Opportunities

Group-based learning opportunities are those in which a group of learners interact with each other and possibly with a subject matter expert, instructor, or source of information to gain the needed knowledge or to develop the desired skills. Examples of group-based learning opportunities are lectures, case studies, facilitated discussions, group simulations, workshops, and other types of team-based collaborative learning situations. Group-based learning usually uses face-to-face communication among the learners and subject matter experts, although technology-based meeting alternatives (for example, IBTV, teleconferencing, collaborative distance communication software) can reduce the need to travel to a central location.

Group-based learning opportunities are probably the most familiar and conventional component of an effective learning environment. Workshops, group discussions, simulations, and lectures are familiar examples of group-based learning opportunities. Well-designed group-based learning is a powerful learning tool. The costs and difficulties associated with assembling a group of learners require sparing use of this alternative.

Criteria for use

Group-based learning opportunities are powerful learning opportunities for the following situations:

- Collaboration among learners is essential for accomplishing the learning objectives. An example is the development and implementation of a new production schedule in a manufacturing plant.

- Learners need to learn volatile content areas, and direct interaction with the creator of the knowledge or a subject matter expert is required. For example, learning about a new product during its formative stages requires access to product design engineers.

- The content is vague and complex and requires a subject matter expert's interpretation. For example, understanding the dynamics of a market segment requires a conversation with a number of experts and experienced colleagues.

- The goal is to help learners develop skills in performing tasks that require teamwork and group decision making. An example is helping learners develop skills in proposal development. Obviously, creating and presenting proposals to customers is not a solitary activity: it involves collaboration and communication among a number of people. The learning experience should resemble the performance situation, so that the learners can interact and make decisions.

Technology-based tools can reduce the costs associated with meeting in a defined time and place. Self-paced learning modules also can complement group-based learning opportunities and reduce their length. The lesson planner should scrutinize the goals of a one-week course to identify any that can be accomplished effectively through self-paced learning modules in order to reduce the group-based section of the course to a one- or two-day session.

Requirements for Successful Implementation of Formal Learning Opportunities

Formal learning opportunities are a crucial component of an effective learning environment. A successful formal learning opportunity includes the following:

- Clear audience descriptions. Members of an organization typically have unique skill development needs. A clear description of the audience, including prerequisites, helps the organization to target and limit the learning options to the appropriate audiences.

- Well-defined learning outcomes and objectives. These should be linked to the tasks that the learners are performing on the job.

- Clearly mapped and sequenced content. Organized content helps learners develop a road map for accomplishing their skill development goals.

- Meaningful linkage of the learning objectives, learning activities, and content. Such connections make it easier for learners to gain the needed skills and knowledge to perform their jobs.

- Clear instructions on how to complete the learning activities and navigate through the content. Students who become confused or lose their place may not successfully complete the training.

- Opportunities within the courseware to practice the skills and apply the knowledge learned. Problem solving within the course allows learners to make sure they have absorbed the new information and can put it to use.

- Opportunities for learners to receive feedback.

- For group-based learning opportunities, an additional requirement concerns the selection of subject matter experts and instructors. These individuals must be well versed in the subject matter, they must be able to approach the subject from multiple vantage points, and they must possess excellent platform delivery skills.

Design Guidelines

An array of formal learning opportunities is an essential component of an effective learning environment. Detailed instruction on how to design and develop formal learning modules is beyond the scope of this book. Many instructional development models (for example, Dills and Romiszowski, 1997; Dick and Carey, 1991) are available. The guidelines summarized in table 3.2 provide a useful checklist for incorporating learning opportunities into an effective learning environment.

Table 3.2: A checklist for designing or selecting formal learning opportunities.

(✓)	Check Off Completed Tasks

☐ 1. Develop a thorough understanding of the employees' work. You can accomplish this informally through reviewing job descriptions, observing performers in the context of their jobs, and engaging in dialogues with the performers about their jobs. A more formal approach uses front-end analysis models and techniques (Rossett, 1987). The approach depends on the complexity and novelty of the job.

☐ 2. Identify and list the skills and knowledge needed to complete the work.

☐ 3. Select the skills and knowledge that the learner will best develop through formal learning opportunities. Differentiate between skills that the learner will best develop through group-based versus self-paced learning modules. Make a list or chart separating skills into the appropriate learning categories.

☐ 4. Define the desired learning objectives and outcomes of every learning activity. Learning objectives should clearly state what the learner should be able to do upon the completion of the activities and the standard that the learner should meet.

☐ 5. Select appropriate content for each learning module and organize the content effectively (see *The Systematic Design of Instruction* by Dick and Carey, 1991).

☐ 6. Select the most appropriate media (audio, video, computer-assisted instruction, text-based instruction, or multimedia) and method (lecture, demonstration, role-playing exercise, or case study). (See *Instructional Media and Technologies for Learning* by Heinich et al., 1996).

☐ 7. Design the learning modules in such a way that they

  • provide frequent practice and feedback opportunities in a controlled environment

  • provide real-world examples and case studies

  • include opportunities to develop and integrate technical and professional skills (for example, to develop technical selling skills, learners need opportunities to find a technical solution, practice negotiating with customers, and prepare and give a presentation).

☐ 8. Ensure that those responsible for defining, developing, and facilitating learning events are experts and experienced practitioners. Facilitator credibility and real-world experience are crucial for the success of this type of learning.

☐ 9. Provide guidelines on how to assemble and package learning modules to create cohesive learning opportunities. Such opportunities can help learners effectively develop clusters of interrelated skills and knowledge.

Summary

Formal learning opportunities constitute the building blocks of an effective learning environment. They provide learners with a variety of learning options from which to select. Well-designed, group-based learning opportunities provide learners with a powerful learning tool. Such opportunities enable learners to collaborate with each other, to interpret vague and complex content information, and to practice group decision making and consensus building. They are, however, expensive and logistically difficult to manage. Their use should balance with self-paced learning opportunities. Learners have the flexibility to use these modularized, self-contained, and technology-based opportunities whenever and wherever they need. Table 3.3 summarizes the criteria for the appropriate use of formal learning opportunities.

Table 3.3: Criteria for selecting formal learning opportunities.

Learning Opportunities	Appropriate for Use When...
Self-paced	• Learning outcomes are well defined • Content is well bounded • Employee can accomplish learning objectives independently • Need for collaboration with another learner or subject matter expert is minimal
Group-based	• Collaboration among learners is essential • Content area is volatile and requires direct interaction with subject matter expert • Content is vague and complex and requires a subject matter expert's interpretation • Employees need to develop skills in teamwork and group decision making

4
Information and Experience Sharing

Opportunities for sharing information and experience allow employees to obtain the latest information and to access their colleagues' and other experts' experience-based knowledge. In contrast to formal learning opportunities, which are used for building foundation skills, these sharing opportunities help learners to

- reinforce existing skills and knowledge
- stay current with new developments that impact their work
- revise skills and knowledge in light of advances or new directions affecting products, tools, processes, or an organization's strategies
- access experience-based knowledge as soon as it becomes available.

These opportunities require active learners. The learners themselves must seek, obtain, and process late-breaking information. They must make the necessary connections among pieces of information, communicate with their colleagues, and contribute to the general pool of understanding.

Information- and experience-sharing opportunities fall into two broad categories: event driven and continuous.

Event-Driven Information and Experience Sharing

In event-driven opportunities for sharing information and experience, a group of learners assemble during a predefined time period. They may analyze and discuss ideas, dissect solutions, or study trends and their implications for current practice. These events can be highly structured with a predefined agenda, such as a forum or panel discussion, or they may be spontaneous, such as a brainstorming brown bag session. They can be "virtual" events, as in an Internet-based chat session, or they can be on-location events in a predetermined place. Table 4.1 shows examples of event-driven information and experience sharing.

Table 4.1: Examples of event-driven information and experience sharing.

	Structured Events	Spontaneous Events
On-location Events	• Forums on industry trends and product plans of an organization • Symposiums on customer needs and expectations • Conferences on evolving technologies • Customer advisory sessions to obtain information from user groups	• Brown bag sessions offered by members of a group on their experiences in completing a complex project at a customer site • Monthly breakfast meetings with the management team to exchange information on organizational developments
Virtual Events	• IBTV program to provide information on major organizational initiatives or shifts in strategic directions of an organization • Regularly scheduled conference calls among members of a distributed product development team to share information on changing requirements in a dynamic market segment	• Conference calls among colleagues to provide information on competitive products and discuss their impact on the organization's product • An online chat session to discuss customer requirements and expectations

In the example of the medical equipment manufacturing company cited in chapter 2, the following information- and experience-sharing events were created as a part of the effective learning environment for the sales force:

- Quarterly forums. In these forums, industry experts presented the evolving customer needs and expectations, product managers presented their product plans to meet the evolving customer needs, and members of sales teams discussed the implications of these proposed new products for their current and future customers.

- Monthly conference calls. For six months after the introduction of a new product, the sales force would have a monthly conference call every third Wednesday of the month to hear the experiences of their colleagues who had successfully sold the product. The conference calls also provided the sales force with an opportunity to ask questions and develop a better understanding of the nuances of selling the new product.

- Weekly brown bag sessions. Every Friday, the local sales offices would serve lunch and sponsor a one-hour information-sharing session in which members of the sales office shared their most recent experiences in positioning the products against competition. In some sessions, guest speakers provided information on various competitors and their strategies.

- Interactive Broadcasting Television events. For major events, such as forging an alliance with a partner, launching a new product line, or implementing major organizational changes, an IBTV session was scheduled. The goal of these sessions was to provide uniform information to the sales force and give them an opportunity to ask questions and discuss the impact of the changes on their accounts.

Continuous Information and Experience Sharing

These opportunities are available continuously to learners who are seeking information and who want to access their colleagues' experience and knowledge. Unlike event-driven opportunities, which require a group of learners to assemble during a predefined time interval, continuous information- and experience-sharing opportunities can take place at any time. Learners use an existing infrastructure, such as a mail and messaging system, to obtain the information and knowledge that they need. They can contact experienced colleagues personally and tap into their expertise, or they can explore sources of information, such as an intranet-based database of specific known problems and solutions. Learners do not have to wait for a scheduled meeting to obtain the needed information. Trainers can package and disseminate the information and knowledge or otherwise make it available for the learners to access and use whenever they need it.

In the sales organization example cited in chapter 2, members of the sales force prepared summary sheets on the problems that they experienced in the course of a sales engagement. These summary sheets, called "knowledge bites," included information on the problem, the context of the problem, possible solutions, and the sales person's insight into preventing or solving the problem in the future. See table 4.2 for the template used by the sales force to prepare knowledge bites. The knowledge bites were stored and made available through the sales intranet site. The sales force members could search the knowledge bites for problems similar to the ones that they were facing and contact the sales representatives for additional information and insight.

Continuous information- and experience-sharing opportunities can be divided into three categories—people based, prepackaged, and on demand. See table 4.3 for examples of continuous information and experience sharing.

People-based continuous information and experience sharing

A human connection must be established to obtain the needed information. In the sales organization example, the sales force could seek and share information on an electronic notes conference. For example, to locate someone to provide a reference for responding to a request for pro-

Table 4.2: Template for preparing knowledge bites.

Needed Information	Instruction
Date	Enter the date of the experience.
Customer	State customer's name and provide a snapshot of the company.
Problem	Clearly state the problem that you faced in selling the product.
Context of the problem	Provide information on the context of the problem. Was the problem related to the product, the competition, or the customer?
Problem resolution	Did you solve the problem? If yes, briefly describe the solution. If no, how do you think this problem should be solved?
Lessons learned	Reflect on your experience and share the lessons that you learned. For example: • If you faced the same problem again, how would you solve it? • What should be done to prevent the problem from happening?
Contacts	Provide the name, phone number, and e-mail address of people who can provide additional information and insight.

Table 4.3: Examples of continuous experience and information sharing.

People based	Prepackaged	On demand
• Face-to-face contact • E-mail • Voicemail • Electronic notes files and bulletin boards • Online charts	• Memos • White papers • Reports • Newsletters • Job aids • Guidelines • Advisory packages • Checklists	• Internet, intranet, and extranet • Databases with a search engine

posal, a sales representative posted questions in the notes conference. The moderator of the notes conference reviewed the notes and sent questions via e-mail to appropriate sales representatives to ensure a timely response to requests for information. All members of the work group could also read and respond to the questions. Another example is the directory published by the sales organization that contained a list of experts and experienced employees in different groups. The sales representatives could call or meet with these employees and take advantage of their expertise in their own sales engagements.

Prepackaged continuous information and experience sharing

Knowledgeable employees, with the help of information designers, capture, package, and disseminate information in this category to learners. Examples are memos, white papers, newsletters, and job aids. Prepackaged information can be available in a variety of formats, for example, electronic, hard copy, or CD-ROM. In the sales organization example, a sales advisory package was created for every new product release. This package contained the following information categories:

- product description (including features, functions, and benefits)
- sales and pricing strategy and recommendations
- target customer information (including customer profile, needs, requirements, business problems, and purchasing strategy)
- reference accounts (including customer profile, business problem solved, customer benefits, and customer testimonials)
- competitor profiles.

The members of the sales force received the package of information and could use the relevant parts when they needed to. "Cheat sheets," created by members of a sales group, illustrate the value of this approach. These sheets summarize members' experiences and provide useful tips for their colleagues. See tables 4.4 and 4.5 for templates generated from cheat sheets created by the sales force.

Table 4.4: A template for creating a product-positioning cheat sheet.

Information Areas (Instruction for creating the cheat sheet)	New Product	Competing Product 1	Competing Product 2	Competing Product 3
Features (list product features)				
Functions (list product functions)				
Benefits (list benefits of the product to customer)				
Price (provide pricing information)				
Total cost of ownership (list the total cost for all products)				
Customer concerns (list potential customer concerns regarding the features, functions, benefits, and total costs as related to each competitive product)				
Overcoming customer objections (list tips on how to address customer concerns originating from competitive products)				

Table 4.4 illustrates a template generated from the first cheat sheet. The sheet features a table created by a sales person to list the features and functions of a product and to compare them with the features and functions of three competitors' products. The table also contains tips on how to overcome customers' concerns when comparing the product with the competition. The cheat sheet illustrated in table 4.5 includes a list of tips on how to avoid mistakes when positioning the new product in a competitive situation with a new customer. The tips are based on the sales person's experience during the first three months of selling the new product

Table 4.5: A template for creating a cheat sheet on sales pitfalls in a competitive setting.

Mistakes and Pitfalls	Impact and Consequences	How to Avoid Mistake or Pitfall
List mistakes that can occur in competitively positioning this product (for example, competing on the price of the product).	List the possible impact and consequences of the mistake (for example, customer might select the product with lower sales price).	List actions that the sales person can take to avoid this mistake. For example, compete on the total cost of ownership, given the fact that the new product has a longer warranty contract and is compatible with the other products, eliminating the need for training.

and on follow-up conversations with customers, in both successful and unsuccessful sales engagements. Members of the sales force received these cheat sheets by electronic mail as soon as they became available.

On-demand continuous information and experience sharing

Information in this category is captured, organized, and then placed in a repository. It is available to the users via an easy-to-use interface and a robust and effective search engine. Depending on their needs, employees can search and access the desired information just in time. The knowledge bites example cited earlier in this chapter illustrates this method.

Each of these continuous opportunities for sharing information and experience requires a different focus. The focus of the people-based method is to provide both an infrastructure (such as a mail and messaging system) and a support system (knowledgeable colleagues who are willing to share their expertise). The infrastructure and support system are necessary to enable learners to contact their colleagues and obtain the needed information and wisdom in a personalized way. Faced with an ill-defined or complex problem, professionals need to be able to contact their colleagues as needed. They may use a colleague as a sounding board, tap into the experience-based knowledge of a colleague, or collaboratively build knowledge for the first time.

The focus for both prepackaged and on-demand methods is on capturing, organizing, and packaging the information or experience-based knowledge as soon as it becomes available and then making it continuously available. The difference between the two methods is that trainers push prepackaged information to the learner but make on-demand information accessible for the learner to use when he or she needs it.

Criteria for Use

Information- and experience-sharing opportunities are desirable components of an effective learning environment in the following circumstances:

- The information and knowledge is experience based, and it does not exist in a structured and conventional format, such as a course on a subject, an article, or a book. In many cases, the information exists only in the minds of practitioners and the creators of the information.
- The work environment is continuously changing. In such an environment, information can lose its currency in a short time and must be shared immediately.
- The information and knowledge are volatile and incomplete. Subject matter experts or successful practitioners need to interpret and analyze such information.

Requirements for Success

Certain conditions must exist to ensure the success of information- and experience-sharing opportunities. See table 4.6 for success requirements of event-driven and continuous opportunities.

Design Guidelines

Certain design guidelines are essential to creating effective information- and experience-sharing opportunities. The guidelines for event-driven and continuous opportunities are somewhat different.

Guidelines for creating event-driven opportunities

Event-driven opportunities for sharing information and experience include forums on industry trends, workshops with subject matter experts,

Table 4.6: Success requirements of information- and experience-sharing opportunities.

Success Factors	Your Actions to Ensure Success
Event-driven opportunities	
Relevance of content	Ensure that the event features relevant trends, developments, topics, and experts in the technical, business, and industry environments.
Credibility of presenters	Ensure that the events feature experts who are known in their fields and who have high credibility to present and guide discussion.
Accessibility to nonlocal employees	Ensure availability of communication technology to enable employees to participate in events through teleconferencing and other tools.
Rewards for participation	Support and encourage employees to participate actively by establishing a reward structure.
Continuous opportunities	
Support infrastructure (such as online forums, a reliable mail and messaging system, an intranet-based information repository, and a search engine)	Invest in the needed infrastructure to ensure • effective exchange of information and experience-based knowledge • collection and dissemination of that information and knowledge as soon as it becomes available.
Information creation and dissemination processes	Use mechanisms that actively capture, organize, and disseminate new information and experience.
Rewards for participation	Support and encourage employees to participate actively.

and prescheduled online chats. Design guidelines concern both what topics to include and how to manage the event itself. The guidelines summarized in table 4.7 provide a checklist for incorporating information- and experience-sharing events into an effective learning environment.

Guidelines for creating continuous opportunities

Guidelines for creating continuous opportunities for sharing information and experience relate either to the infrastructure or to the culture of the organization.

Infrastructure. The infrastructure comprises tools and technologies as well as practices and procedures. Tools and technologies include system, network, and telecommunications resources that enable continuous communication among employees. Some examples are electronic mail, conference

Table 4.7: Checklist for designing event-driven information- and experience-sharing opportunities.

(✓) Check Off Completed Tasks

Select appropriate topics:

☐ Research industry literature and consult knowledgeable individuals for trends, issues, innovations, and experts that are judged to have significant impact on current work.

☐ Obtain input from members of the work group to identify topics that are of interest.

☐ Select and prioritize topics of interest based on business objectives, input from knowledgeable employees, or the interest of the audience.

Manage the event:

☐ Determine the format most appropriate to the subject and resource constraints. Possibilities include product demonstrations, seminars, panel discussions, paper presentations followed by questions and answers, online facilitated chats, and regularly scheduled conference calls.

☐ Assess speaker or facilitator candidates for their availability and credibility with the audience and enlist strong candidates for participation.

☐ Work with line managers to schedule events so that the highest number of people can attend with the lowest impact on work.

☐ Work with those who manage the physical plant to ensure appropriate seating capacity and delivery media, such as projectors, a video player, or a white board.

☐ Make necessary arrangements with system administrators and telecommunications personnel to make sure that telephone lines are available for conference calls and that system and networking resources are available for online chats and the exchange of ideas.

☐ Work with facilitators and speakers to ensure that they are adequately prepared and correctly target information to meet audience needs.

☐ Capture and record events in a written narrative or on videotape.

☐ Evaluate each event using surveys or exit interviews. Events themselves provide opportunities to identify additional topics for future events and preferred delivery strategies.

calls, and online forums. Tools and technologies also include databases or intranet-based information repositories with search capabilities. These technologies store information and experience-based knowledge as it becomes available and enable employees to search, access, and use that information.

Specific practices and procedures enable trainers to identify, collect, organize, package, and continuously update needed information and experience-based knowledge as it becomes available. The guidelines summarized in table 4.8 provide a checklist for creating an infrastructure for continuous information- and experience-sharing opportunities.

Table 4.8: Checklist for designing continuous information- and experience-sharing opportunities.

(✓) Check Off Completed Tasks

Create the tools and technologies component of an infrastructure:

❏ Select appropriate methods for sharing information and experience, such as an employee forum, an intranet-based sales advisory, or a database to record problems and solutions for a service work group.

❏ Identify the needed infrastructure to implement the selected methods. Some examples are intranet access or a distribution technique for disseminating sales advisory packages and updating them regularly.

❏ Study the existing infrastructure to determine whether it accommodates the new requirements. If possible, try to utilize the existing infrastructure instead of investing time and resources in building a new one.

❏ Define necessary adjustments to the existing infrastructure and identify new aspects of the infrastructure that must be built.

❏ Engage and build appropriate alliances with individuals and departments responsible for the infrastructure, including information systems, telecommunications, and distribution departments and Internet service providers. Make the necessary arrangements to ensure availability and accessibility of the needed infrastructure.

Create the practices and procedures component of an infrastructure:

❏ Establish a process for identifying the information and experience domains that are most valuable to the work group by continuously assessing and validating the information and experience-based knowledge needs of the group.

❏ Identify one individual to be responsible for each information and experience domain. This person is responsible for obtaining, synthesizing, and updating information and for making information available. He or she can solicit help and support from knowledgeable colleagues in synthesizing and distributing information. Managers should measure this employee's work by the availability, accuracy, and accessibility of the information.

❏ Adopt a set of guidelines for capturing, formatting, storing, and disseminating information.

For most organizations, an intranet is the most appropriate foundation for disseminating information continuously and for sharing experience. An intranet-based system enables workers to

- store and disseminate information in different formats—text, graphics, audio, and video
- store source files (for example, Microsoft Word, Excel, PowerPoint) as well as processed information files (for example, text, PostScript)
- conduct customized searches based on criteria defined by the users
- integrate internal and external sources of information

- eliminate redundant activities for disseminating information
- update the information frequently
- make the latest information immediately available.

Culture. When creating continuous opportunities for sharing information and experience, one must address both the infrastructure and cultural issues. There are many definitions for organizational culture. After reviewing a wide array of definitions, Robbins (1990) uncovered a central theme and stated that *organizational culture* refers to "a system of shared meaning." Organizational culture includes "patterns of beliefs, symbols, rituals, myths, and practices that have evolved over time." These patterns create a set of expectations and determine how members of an organization should behave. The success of the information-sharing component of an effective learning environment depends to a great extent on the active participation of employees and their willingness to share their knowledge and information with others. The culture of the organization should encourage this behavior. Establishing effective information- and experience-sharing opportunities is difficult in an organization whose climate is characterized by distrust, a lack of cooperation among co-workers, and a reward system that encourages competition and rewards individual rather than group achievements. For these organizations, changing this cultural climate is the crucial first step in the successful implementation of this component of an effective learning environment. The change requires a systemic approach. The organization must make a focused and multifaceted effort to do the following:

- Set expectations around willingness to share information. Robbins (1990) believes that responsibility for establishing and communicating new expectations in an organization lies with the top management. The leaders and managers must articulate the value of reciprocal information sharing and clearly communicate this business imperative to the employees. See Kochan and Useem (1992) for more details on how to establish new expectations in an organization.

- Establish a new contract with new and current employees encouraging sharing of information and knowledge. In the sales organization example cited in chapter 2, the managers communicated to the sales force that active participation in information and experience sharing is an integral part of each employee's job. Managers stated their expectations that all employees learn continuously and contribute actively to the skill development of their colleagues. Sales managers agreed to add an information-sharing goal to the goal sheet of each sales representative.

- Make information and experience sharing an integral component of everyone's job, and measure and reward everyone accordingly. In the sales organization example, to ensure active participation of the sales force in information and experience sharing, the organization changed its performance review forms to include a section on active participation in creating knowledge bites, teaching brown bag sessions, participating in monthly conference calls, and responding to colleagues' questions posted in the notes conference.

- Establish the right reward system to encourage the right behavior. In the sales organization example, creating the knowledge bites encouraged the sales force to reflect on their experiences and to capture their learning. Creating a knowledge bite became a requirement for gaining credit for closing a sale. A reward and recognition program was created to encourage the sales force to share their experience-based knowledge actively.

- Provide appropriate behavioral models at all levels of the organization to encourage openness and information sharing. In the sales example, the sales managers modeled information-sharing behavior. They created knowledge bites that reflected their experiences, reviewed knowledge bites created by account teams and contacted them for follow-up information, and participated in the quarterly forums.

Keep in mind that cultural change of this type does not take place overnight. Change requires significant time to take hold.

Summary

Information and experience sharing is a crucial component of an effective learning environment in contemporary organizations that face the challenge of providing their employees with the latest information and access to experience-based knowledge. It allows organizations to meet the challenge of continuous changes in the required skill set, as experts can share the most up-to-date information as soon as that information becomes available. Information and experience sharing is not usually used for building foundation skills, but instead for expanding learners' understanding, updating their information, and helping them explore nuances of meaning. Whether event driven or continuous, the sharing of information and experience requires a cooperative and open organizational culture. It also requires an efficient and easy-to-use process for creating, storing, disseminating, accessing, and updating information. Continuous information- and experience-sharing opportunities require, in addition, an infrastructure of tools and technology. These opportunities are appropriate when information is based on experience, when it exists only in practitioners' minds, when the work environment is continuously changing, or when the information is volatile and incomplete.

5

Development Opportunities

Development opportunities are structured, on-the-job learning interventions developed for individual learners. Three types of development opportunities exist in an effective learning environment—mentoring, cognitive apprenticeships, and internships.

- Mentoring socializes learners to the larger context of an organization, profession, or industry. The employee works one-on-one with a seasoned colleague. For example, a sales professional might enter a mentoring relationship to develop an understanding of the sociopolitical considerations involved in selling products or services to executives in senior management.

- Cognitive apprenticeships help learners to develop a complex set of cognitive skills—such as decision making or problem solving—under the supervision of an expert performer. For example, a less experienced instructional designer might enter into a cognitive apprenticeship with an expert instructional designer to develop skills in defining the performance improvement needs of an organization and in proposing learning solutions to improve business performance.

- Internships help learners to develop a thorough understanding of the best practices of a host organization through immersion in another organization, either internal or external. For example, to develop advanced skills in servicing a product, a service delivery professional might spend time in a product-engineering group. Or a business development manager who is responsible for launching a new product in a targeted market segment might spend time in another organization that has extensive experience in successfully launching products in that market segment.

Development opportunities can help an organization deal effectively with several of the factors that create the challenge in skill development and maintenance: skill complexity, lack of resident expertise, lack of uniformity in skill deficiency among employees, and a dynamic workforce. The following section details how development opportunities can address each factor.

Complexity of the Required Skill Set

To meet business challenges, employees need to develop complex sets of skills, such as abilities in building a relationship of trust with customers, designing a retirement investment plan, configuring a secure client-to-server computing environment, interviewing a potential job applicant, or approving a business loan application. Development of these complex skill sets is a process rather than an event: it requires immersion in a real-world situation, a mentoring relationship with an experienced colleague, or a cognitive apprenticeship with an expert performer. Development opportunities provide reality-based learning experiences that are conducive to the development of complex skill sets.

Lack of Resident Expertise

As an organization establishes complicated partnerships with other organizations, develops complex products and services, or enters new market segments, the needed expertise to develop and deliver learning solutions for its employees may no longer exist in the organization. The service organization cited in the chapter 1 example became a service provider for products of other partner companies. The needed product knowledge no longer existed within the internal engineering community. To help the service professionals develop the skills to support the new products, the organization went beyond its boundaries and tapped into the expertise and learning opportunities in the partner company. In the sales organization example cited in chapter 2, the company decided to introduce a new, complex product in a brand-new market segment. The sales force had to compete against several entrenched competitors for the first time, and its members did not have any experience in selling to that market segment. Furthermore, the complexity of the product required consultative selling. The organization arranged a three- to five-week internship program through which selected members of the sales force spent time in the sales organization of one of its customers. This customer had extensive experience in consultative selling in that market segment. This program was extremely beneficial to the sales force. Internships and sabbaticals are powerful development opportunities that help organizations train their employees despite a lack of resident expertise.

Lack of Uniformity in Skill Deficiency Among Employees

Organizations need to individualize learning opportunities to the unique skill development needs of the learners. A major attribute of development options, such as mentoring, cognitive apprenticeships, and internships, is that instructional designers can customize them to the unique skill development needs of individual learners. Traditional training interventions target the average or typical learner, but development opportunities fulfill the unique needs of each learner. Development opportunities are usually one-on-one engagements between an expert or knowledgeable colleague and the learner. In the internship program example cited earlier in this chapter, internship coordinators developed internship agreements for the sales representatives prior to their internship experience. The agreements defined the desired outcome of the internship, its scope, and the needed resources and established a timeline for each internship engagement. The agreements brought a high level of individualization to the internship experience for each employee.

Dynamic Workforce

Organizations face an increasing need to orient the newly hired employees and, at the same time, to tap into their expertise. Mentoring provides an opportunity to introduce newcomers to the larger context of the organization. Through cognitive apprenticeships, newly hired experts can help resident employees develop expertise in new domains. In this way, the development component of an effective learning environment can help an organization cope with a high turnover rate. In the sales organization example, newly hired sales representatives were assigned to a mentor. The mentor's responsibility was twofold:

- to socialize the new employee to the context of the organization
- to help the new employee conduct an assessment of personal skill development needs and guide him or her through the process of formulating a learning and development plan.

Criteria for Use

In an effective learning environment, development opportunities are best suited for teaching complex skill sets that require direct, reality-based learning activities.

Each type of development opportunity is best suited to a particular type of complex skill set. Mentoring socializes a learner to the larger context of an organization, industry, or profession. For example, a recently hired employee can benefit from a mentoring opportunity that enables him or her to learn about the inner workings of an organization.

Cognitive apprenticeships help make explicit the tacit and invisible cognitive skills (such as problem solving and decision making) used by an expert. For example, a junior partner in a law firm can benefit from working closely with a senior partner to determine the merits of a legal case and to learn how to devise a defense strategy after accepting a case.

Where internal expertise is limited, organizations should use internships. Internships provide exposure to an external work environment, full of rich learning opportunities. For example, a manufacturing plant supervisor who will be implementing a multiskilled workforce strategy in his or her plant can benefit from spending a few months in a plant that has successfully implemented the same strategy.

Guidelines for Creating Development Options

Successful implementation of development opportunities requires action and support at the global or organizational level and at the local level.

Global level

The term *global* indicates that this support takes place at the organizational level to ensure consistency and economy of effort. An organization must create a hospitable environment for implementing development options at this global level. The organization must develop the necessary infrastructure, allocate needed resources, make necessary adjustments to the work environment, and provide the required organizational support structure. Table 5.1 provides a sample of activities that an organization must perform at a global level to successfully implement mentoring arrangements, cognitive apprenticeships, and internships.

Local level

The infrastructure, tools, and processes developed at a global level must be put into operation, customized, and implemented at a local level, that is, at the work-group level. The learner and local managers use these resources, tools, and procedures to craft an individualized development opportunity. In the sales example cited in chapter 2, the sales representative, the mentor, and a coordinator worked together to create a mentoring engagement at a local level. They defined the engagement itself, the

Table 5.1: Guidelines for creating development opportunities at a global level.

- Create a process at the organizational level for identifying and creating a pool of mentors and experts and for enlisting their cooperation.
- Create a process and develop a set of criteria for identifying host organizations and for establishing a high-level employee exchange agreement for internship opportunities.
- Create tools and procedures for defining, designing, coordinating, implementing, and evaluating successful development opportunities. Tools include evaluation forms and templates for agreements and status reports. Procedures include creating mentor or master profiles; matching learners' development needs with mentors, experts, or attributes of a host organization; defining and securing needed resources; and terminating an engagement.
- Develop and implement orientation and learning activities to prepare participants for different roles—roles that include mentors, masters, sponsors in the host organization, and learners. See chapters 6 through 8 for more detail.
- Allocate needed resources to encourage participation of experienced and knowledgeable employees. These resources might include giving financial relief to line managers who agree to allow employees to serve as mentors to junior employees.
- Make necessary adjustments in the work environment to accommodate on-the-job learning without compromising the quality of work or service to customers. See chapters 6 through 9 for more detail.
- Establish a reward system to encourage active participation of learners, mentors, experts, and managers. See chapters 6 through 9 for more detail.

desired outcome, and a mentoring strategy, including the time and resources required. They also developed a mentor-protégé agreement, obtained the needed resources, implemented the plans, and later evaluated the mentoring engagement. Finally, they made an attempt to ensure that the mentoring opportunity was fully integrated with other learning options, such as internships and formal learning.

Successful implementation of development opportunities requires that an organization create the needed infrastructure, allocate resources, and institutionalize the appropriate support structure at the global level. The organization must also ensure appropriate use of resources and infrastructure at a local level.

Summary

Development opportunities are structured, on-the-job learning options geared toward individual learners. Three types of development opportunities exist in an effective learning environment—mentoring arrangements, cognitive apprenticeships, and internships.

In an effective learning environment, development opportunities teach complex skill sets that require direct, reality-based learning activities.

6

Mentoring

The following three chapters examine each type of development opportunity (mentoring opportunities, cognitive apprenticeships, and internships) in greater detail and provide guidelines for developing them.

Mentoring is a time-honored professional development method. In the context of an effective learning environment, *mentoring* is defined as a learning opportunity in which an experienced colleague, the *mentor*, socializes the learner or the protégé to the larger context of an organization, profession, or industry. The following activities achieve this socialization:

- helping the protégé develop an understanding of the true workings of the organization, including relationships, workarounds, rules of thumb, and unwritten procedures and practices
- providing the protégé with appropriate contacts in the organization and in the profession
- providing the protégé access to internal and external sources of information, such as strategic plans, market reports, management briefings, journals, and professional associations and activities
- demonstrating values and behaviors desired by the organization and profession by acting as a role model
- acting as a sounding board for the protégé's ideas and providing timely advice.

Examples of circumstances where mentoring is appropriate include the following:

- A newly hired employee wants to develop an understanding of the organization's marketing strategy, practices, and strengths.

- A project manager wants to develop an in-depth understanding of business practices within an organization, such as procurement, contracting, and invoicing.
- A sales professional wants to develop an understanding of internal technical support available to him or her for defining and presenting a solution to customers and wants to learn how to access these resources effectively.

Mentoring as a component of an effective learning environment is somewhat different from most conventional mentoring engagements. Mentoring is primarily a means for socializing the learner to the larger context of the organization. But some mentoring programs are of a broader scope: they cover all aspects of on-the-job training, including apprenticeships, coaching, and internships.

Mentoring is structured, focused, and well bounded. Loosely structured mentoring engagements can be discouraging for the mentor, frustrating for the protégé, and ultimately unsuccessful in tapping the full potential of this development opportunity. To ensure success, learning outcomes, areas of skill and knowledge development, the timeline, and the resources needed must all be well defined and articulated in a mentoring agreement.

Mentoring is structured around a mentor-protégé agreement. This contract serves several purposes. It establishes the working relationship between the mentor and the protégé, it describes expectations and documents commitments, and it provides a structure for the engagement. This contract is a living document for capturing changes throughout the engagement. See figure 6.1 for an example of a mentoring agreement template used in the sales organization example cited in chapter 2.

The skill development needs of a learner may require multiple mentors. A board of mentors may advise the person on different aspects of his or her skill development needs. Using mentors from within and outside the organization can also help ensure an effective mentoring engagement. When multiple mentors are involved, a mentorship coordinator should draw up multiple contracts. Also, depending on the skill development needs of the protégé, the length of the mentoring engagement can vary from weeks to months.

Mentoring requires a coordinator. The coordinator can be the manager, a learning and development professional, or a colleague. The coordinator

Figure 6.1: Mentoring program agreement template.

Protégé: _____

Mentor: _____

Expected Performance Outcome:

[What will the newly hired sales representative be able to do as a result of the mentoring engagement?]

Skills and Knowledge Areas to Develop:

[What skill areas will be the focus of the engagement? Use the results of the sales self-assessment tool.]

Methods and Activities:

[What mentoring methods will the mentor use? Select and describe appropriate methods such as tutoring, informing, role modeling, and advising.]

Protégé Evaluation:

[How will the mentor assess the protégé's skill and knowledge acquisition?]

Engagement Evaluation:

[How will the effectiveness of the engagement be evaluated?]

Resources:

[What resources (for example, special tools and budget) will be needed?]

Duration:

[What is the starting date and how long will the engagement last?]

Frequency and Duration of Meetings:

[How many times and how often will the protégé meet with the mentor?]

Mentor's Time Commitment:

[How many hours will the mentor spend on the engagement-related activities?]

Protégé Time Commitment:

[How many hours will the protégé spend on engagement-related activities?]

Termination Process:

[How will the engagement terminate?]

_____

Signature of Mentor

_____

Signature of Mentor's Manager

_____

Signature of Protégé

_____

Signature of Protégé's Manager

- works with the protégé to define his or her learning and development needs
- identifies and enlists an appropriate number of mentors to help the protégé develop the needed skills
- works with the protégé and the mentor to define the mentoring engagement and participates in preparing the mentoring contract
- enlists management support and ensures allocation of needed resources
- monitors the progress of the mentoring engagement, troubleshoots potential problems, and ensures midcourse correction to encourage a successful engagement
- orients the protégé and mentor and helps them understand their roles, expectations, and resources
- evaluates the success of the mentoring engagement and helps terminate the engagement.

Criteria for Use

The development component of an effective learning environment is best suited for developing complex skill sets, such as building a relationship of trust with customers. Developing these skill sets requires direct, reality-based learning activities. Mentoring as a development technique is recommended in situations such as the following:

- The learner needs to develop an understanding of the true workings of an organization.
- An organization faces an influx of new employees during a period of growth.
- An organization faces a high turnover rate.
- Learning needs of employees are individualized and do not lend themselves to group interventions for skill development.
- An organization is in its formative stages, and processes do not yet exist for completing the work of the organization.

- An organization faces rapid changes and does not have enough time to capture, package, and disseminate organizational know-how.

Requirements

A successful mentoring opportunity requires certain factors:

- Management commitment. Management must create the right climate and allocate needed resources to ensure successful implementation of a mentoring engagement.
- Selection of the right mentors. Mentors must not only be knowledgeable about the true workings of the organization, but also be capable of attending to the learner's needs and able to communicate effectively.
- Protégé commitment. Mentoring requires the learner to demonstrate initiative and to pursue the learning opportunities.
- Mentor-protégé orientation. Orientation establishes expectations and communicates mentoring and feedback techniques.
- Clear definition of the skill development needs of the protégé.
- Mentor commitment in terms of time and the quality of his or her contribution to the engagement.
- A well-articulated mentor-protégé agreement that outlines learning outcomes, needed resources, time commitments, provisions for problem resolution, evaluation processes to ensure the success of the mentoring engagement, and termination processes.

Design Guidelines

Successful mentoring requires a systemic approach to design and implementation, as do the design and implementation of the effective learning environment itself. A series of tasks must be performed at two levels—global and local.

Global tasks

These tasks enable an organization to create a hospitable climate for implementing an effective mentoring engagement. Included tasks are listed below.

Allocating needed resources. Resources needed include

- financial relief for the time that the mentor and protégé commit to the mentoring engagement
- a budget allocated to the protégé for subscribing to journals and paying membership fees to join professional organizations
- funds to cover costs associated with acquiring sources of information (for example, industry trends reports, market reports, management briefings, and professional literature).

Making necessary adjustments to the work environment. These adjustments accommodate on-the-job learning without compromising the quality of work or service to customers.

Establishing a reward system. Such systems encourage active participation of learners, colleagues, and managers.

Developing the necessary infrastructure. The infrastructure includes the tools, processes, and practices needed to implement mentoring successfully. A number of processes should exist at the organizational level and be available for implementation at the local level. These processes should enable those at the local level to answer the following questions:

- How to identify mentors? Organizations can enlist prospective mentors from a variety of internal and external sources. Table 6.1 shows the characteristics needed by a mentor and questions to gauge a prospective mentor's qualifications.
- How to define and assess skill development needs of employees and select skills that mentoring might help to develop? The types of skill sets needed by mentors are described in the "criteria for use" section of this chapter.
- How to identify candidates for a mentoring engagement? A successful mentoring engagement requires a committed learner. Table 6.2 lists necessary learner attributes and questions to measure a prospective protégé's commitment.

Table 6.1: Mentor characteristics.

Attributes	Guiding Questions
Technical competence	Is the mentor technically competent?
Organizational knowledge	Is the mentor well versed in the organization: its goals, strategic directions, culture, practices, operations, and organizational structure?
Industry knowledge	How extensive is this person's knowledge and understanding of the industry?
Willingness to help others	Is the mentor committed to the growth and development of others?
Interpersonal skills	Does the mentor communicate effectively with others?
Perceived status	Is the mentor well respected by colleagues inside and outside the organization?

Table 6.2: Protégé characteristics.

Attributes	Guiding Questions
Personal responsibility for learning	Is the protégé committed to his or her own growth? Does the protégé take initiative to learn? Are learning and skill mastery high priorities for the protégé? Does the protégé have an inquiring mind?
Work habits	Is the protégé capable of working under the guidance and direction of others? Is the protégé organized? Does the protégé manage his or her time effectively?
Interpersonal skills	Does the protégé communicate effectively with others? Does the protégé work well with others? Does the protégé demonstrate empathy toward others?

- How to develop an agreement between the protégé and mentor?
- How to define, design, coordinate, implement, and evaluate successful mentoring engagements?
- How to develop and implement an orientation to prepare mentors and learners for their roles?

Local tasks

Coordinators, with help from learners, must perform a number of tasks at the local level to put the mentoring opportunity in operation. These tasks fall into four groups: planning, implementation, termination, and evaluation. Figure 6.2 depicts the relationship among these four task groups. See table 6.3 for a checklist of tasks performed in each group. The following is a short description of local tasks.

Figure 6.2: A process for creating a development opportunity (such as a mentoring arrangement, a cognitive apprenticeship, or an internship).

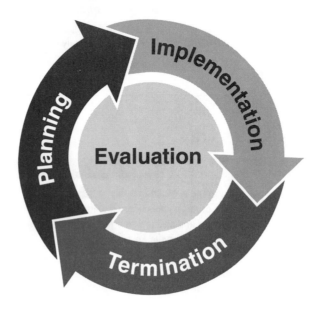

Planning tasks. The first task is determining the skill development needs of the learner. Then the learner and coordinator can determine whether mentoring is an appropriate option. Planning tasks include the following:

- Define the skills and knowledge needed to perform the job.
- Develop assessment tools, either self-assessments or tests, to help learners determine their skill development needs.
- Use the tools to assess an individual's skill development needs either formally, using tests or self-assessment tools, or informally, using anecdotal recommendations by colleagues or the individual's subjective assessments.
- Identify any skill and knowledge areas that are best addressed by mentoring.

Table 6.3: Checklist of tasks performed at a local level to design and employ mentoring and cognitive apprenticeships.

Task Groups	(✓) Check Off Completed Tasks
Planning	**Determine skill development needs:** ❏ Define the skills needed to perform the job. ❏ Develop skill assessment tools. ❏ Assess individuals' skill development needs. ❏ Identify skill areas that are best taught by mentoring or apprenticeship. **Select mentors or experts:** ❏ Define a set of criteria for selecting mentors or experts. ❏ Search for potential candidates who meet the criteria. ❏ Create a pool of potential mentors or experts. ❏ Match characteristics of the mentors or experts with the learners'. ❏ Select and enlist the mentors or experts. **Develop an agreement:** ❏ Define the scope of the engagement. ❏ Define the desired outcomes. ❏ Identify the appropriate activities. ❏ Identify the needed resources. ❏ Define timelines. ❏ Identify requirements.
Implementing	**Orient the mentor or expert and the learner:** ❏ Train the mentor or expert and the learner on the engagement process. ❏ Help the mentor or expert and the learner understand their roles. ❏ Train the mentor or expert and the learner on mentoring or cognitive apprenticeship techniques. **Implement the agreement:** ❏ Resolve problems. ❏ Adapt engagement to emerging needs.
Terminating	❏ Monitor progress. ❏ Terminate the process upon accomplishment of the objectives.
Evaluating	❏ Evaluate how well the engagement accomplished the learning objectives. ❏ Evaluate the appropriateness of the engagement.

Once you have identified what it is that employees need to learn and have determined that mentoring is the best way to answer that need, you can begin to identify mentors. The following list of tasks makes identifying, selecting, and enlisting appropriate mentors possible. The coordinator, in consultation with the learners and potential mentors, performs these tasks:

- Defines a set of criteria for selecting mentors.
- Searches for internal and external potential candidates who meet the criteria.
- Creates a pool of potential mentors.
- Matches characteristics of the mentors with the learners'.
- Selects the mentors.
- Negotiates with the mentors and their managers to enlist their support and gain their commitment.

A mentoring agreement defines the scope, activities, outcomes, needed resources, timelines, and other requirements of a mentoring engagement. (See table 7.1, page 73, for the elements of a mentoring or cognitive apprenticeship agreement.)

Implementation tasks. Orientation is the link between planning and implementation. Orientation helps the mentor and protégé develop an understanding of their roles and expectations, as well as a familiarity with mentoring techniques. Orientation activities are crucial to the success of mentoring. Mentoring is different from traditional teaching and learning techniques. Mentors need to learn specific mentoring techniques and the protégé needs to learn specific techniques for learning. The mentor and protégé need to develop a relationship within the engagement guidelines and to learn how the mentoring engagement should work. The coordinator is typically quite involved in the orientation. In the sales organization mentoring program example, a half-day orientation workshop and a mentoring handbook were prepared and delivered to mentor and protégé teams. An outline of the mentoring workshop appears in table 6.4.

Mentoring activities consist of techniques used by the mentor to help the protégé develop the needed skills and knowledge. These techniques include

- Tutoring. The mentor helps the protégé develop an understanding of the true workings of the organization, such as relationships, workarounds, rules of thumb, and unwritten procedures and practices.

- Providing exposure. The mentor provides the protégé appropriate contacts in the organization and profession.

- Informing. The mentor provides the protégé access to internal and external sources of information (for example, strategic plans, market reports, management briefings, journals, and professional associations and activities).

- Role modeling. By acting as a role model, the mentor demonstrates values and behaviors desired by the organization and profession.

- Advising. The mentor acts as a sounding board for the protégé's ideas and provides timely advice.

The protégé also uses specific techniques:

- Researching. Through researching, the protégé plays an active role in his or her own learning; and the protégé follows the leads provided by the mentor to seek, obtain, analyze, and synthesize information.

Table 6.4: Outline of the mentoring orientation workshop.

Elements	Description
Audience	Mentor and protégé
Length	Half day
Objectives	Mentor and protégé should be able to • demonstrate an understanding of the mentoring process, relationship, and roles and responsibilities • use mentoring techniques such as tutoring, providing exposure, informing, role modeling, and advising • prepare and implement a mentoring agreement • terminate the mentoring engagement and evaluate its effectiveness.
Instructional strategy	A combination of lecture, discussion, and role-playing will help the audience accomplish the learning objectives.
Topics	• Mentoring (definition, roles, expectation) • Mentoring process (tools and templates) • Mentoring techniques • How to prepare a mentoring contract • How to implement a successful mentoring engagement • How to assess the effectiveness of a mentoring engagement

- Practicing. Practicing enables the protégé to use newly gained skills and awareness under the mentor's supervision.
- Seeking advice. Seeking advice enables the protégé to use the mentor as a sounding board for his or her ideas.

Termination tasks. As a component of an effective learning environment, mentoring is not an open-ended engagement. The protégé's progress toward accomplishing the goal is monitored by the protégé, the mentor, and the coordinator. Upon accomplishment of the mentoring goals, the engagement is formally terminated.

Evaluation tasks. Evaluation is ongoing throughout the mentoring engagement. Evaluation tasks determine the effectiveness of the mentoring process and assess the degree to which the learner accomplishes the learning objectives. Evaluation can sometimes make it clear that the mentoring is not working well. In most cases, a midcourse correction can ensure the success of the engagement. Both the mentor and the protégé perform evaluation tasks. Table 6.5 lists areas for focus and questions to evaluate the mentoring in those areas.

Table 6.5: Areas of evaluation.

Areas for Focus	Guiding Questions
Mentor/protégé match	Were the mentor and protégé an appropriate match?
Commitment	Were the mentor, the protégé, and their managers committed to the success of the engagement?
Orientation	Was the orientation adequate to help the protégé and mentor develop an understanding of their roles, responsibilities, and the mentoring techniques?
Resources	Were the required resources (time, tools, and information) allocated sufficient?
Mentoring activities	• Were sufficient work-related activities and experiences available for practice and exposure? • Were meetings between the mentor and protégé timely and productive? • Was sufficient flexibility built into the engagement to ensure its meaningfulness?
Duration	Was the duration of the engagement appropriate for meeting the protégé's development needs?

Summary

Mentoring is a powerful development technique that can socialize the learner to the larger context of an organization. Mentoring, as a component of an effective learning environment, is well structured and bounded. It is based on a mentor-protégé agreement. Mentoring works best when it is integrated with other development opportunities, such as cognitive apprenticeships and internships, and with other components of an effective learning environment, such as formal learning and experience and information sharing.

Detailed guidelines on developing mentoring engagements are beyond the scope of this book. Readers are encouraged to review the references at the back of this book for information on how to define and implement an effective mentoring engagement.

7

Cognitive Apprenticeships

A cognitive apprenticeship is an on-the-job learning situation in which an expert practitioner helps a colleague—apprentice or learner—develop complex cognitive skills. The focus of cognitive apprenticeships, as opposed to that of traditional apprenticeships, is on invisible cognitive tasks, such as problem solving or decision making. (In traditional apprenticeships, the focus is on physical tasks, such as operating a machine or building a product.) Cognitive apprenticeships share the following attributes with traditional apprenticeships:

- The learner starts with simple tasks and progresses toward more complex tasks as his or her competence emerges naturally and continuously.

- Teaching is invisible. Learning takes place in the context of the work, and the learner develops the needed skills while working with the expert.

- The expert's performance constitutes the standard for the apprentice.

- Apprenticeship is used to initiate the learner into the community of expert performers.

Cognitive apprenticeships bring the expert's tacit thought processes and associated knowledge into the open, where the learner can observe, enact, and practice them. In this way, implicit understandings gained from experience transfer from expert to learner. Cognitive apprenticeships help learners to integrate and apply subskills and theoretical knowledge learned through other components of an effective learning environment. Cognitive apprenticeships encourage a deeper understanding of other learning and tie concepts more closely to their application in the work context.

In cognitive apprenticeships, according to Collins, et al. (1991), an expert or master performer works with the learner using methods such as modeling, coaching, scaffolding, articulation, reflection, and exploration. (These methods are described in the implementation section of this chapter.) The expert chooses tasks to illustrate the application of specific skills and knowledge, to give learners practice in applying them in diverse settings, and to increase the complexity of tasks slowly so that component skills can be integrated. The expert selects tasks that reflect the changing demands of the situation.

For example, an expert in planning investments for college education might work with a learner to help him or her explore the conceptual knowledge and processes involved in preparing an investment plan for a family. In the sales organization example, successful and experienced sales representatives helped their colleagues learn to

- interpret customers' needs, requirements, issues, problems, and questions
- recognize customers' priorities, needs, and expectations
- define a solution that meets customers' requirements.

The following are additional examples of work for which cognitive apprenticeships can be an effective skill development technique:

- planning, monitoring, and controlling complex projects
- forecasting, tracking, and controlling a budget for an organization
- using seemingly unrelated data to reach a solution
- reviewing the facts of a case to determine whether a contract has been broken.

As a component of an effective learning environment, cognitive apprenticeships have attributes similar to those of internships. Cognitive apprenticeships are structured, focused, and well bounded. Learning outcomes, areas of skill and knowledge development, the timeline, and needed resources are all well defined. Cognitive apprenticeships are based on an agreement between the learner and the expert. This agreement establishes the working relationship between the learner and the expert, describes expectations, documents commitments, and provides a structure for the engagement. See table 7.1 for a list of mentoring and cognitive apprenticeship agreement items.

Table 7.1: Elements of a mentoring or cognitive apprenticeship agreement.

Elements	Guiding Questions
Expected performance outcome	What will the learner be able to do as a result of the engagement?
Skill and knowledge areas to develop	What skill and knowledge areas will be the focus of the engagement?
Methods and activities	What methods will the mentor or expert use to help the learner develop the needed skills and knowledge?
Learner evaluation	How will the mentor or expert assess the learner's skill and knowledge acquisition?
Engagement evaluation	How will the effectiveness of the engagement be evaluated? (Possible options are meetings or evaluation forms.)
Resources	What resources will be needed, for example, special tools (such as videotape to capture expert and learner interaction with clients) or budget?
Duration	What is the starting date, and how long will the engagement last?
Frequency of meetings	How many times and how often will the learner meet with the mentor or expert?
Expert's time commitment	How many hours will the mentor or expert spend preparing for meetings, meeting with the learner, and participating in engagement-related activities?
Learner's time commitment	How many hours will the learner spend preparing for meetings, meeting with the mentor or expert, and participating in engagement-related activities?
Special arrangements	Are there any unique requirements for this engagement? (For example, will the expert set guidelines regarding work on customer projects or spell out possible areas of potential conflict of interest and how to handle them?)
Termination process	How will the engagement be terminated? Is a formal appraisal needed? Should the mentor or expert and learner prepare a report?
Signature	Have those involved (mentor, expert, learner, and their managers) signed the agreement?

A cognitive apprenticeship may require multiple experts. Different experts may be needed for different skill development needs of the learner. For instance, a sales executive may be an "expert" for a sales professional who is preparing to take on a major account responsibility. The same sales professional might work with a different expert to improve his or her skills in matching customer business problems with the solutions offered by the corporation. When multiple experts are involved, multiple contracts are necessary. Also, the length of the apprenticeship varies. The length depends on the skill development needs of the learner. A coordinator must set up the engagement, manage its progress, obtain needed resources, and evaluate its success. See chapter 6 for a more complete description of the coordinator's role.

Criteria for Use

Cognitive apprenticeships, like other development techniques, are best suited for developing complex skill sets requiring direct, reality-based learning activities. They are recommended in situations like the following:

- The learner needs to develop an in-depth understanding of a complex knowledge domain as it applies to real-world situations (for example, preparing a college investment plan for the children of a young couple or matching the plan to their lifestyle and investment timeline).
- An organization wants to make the tacit knowledge of its experts explicit to its members. For example, a management consulting firm wants junior partners to develop skills in planning, monitoring, and controlling large-scale, complex, and global projects.
- An organization wants to create a community of experts and initiate new members into the community. In the computer service organization example cited in chapter 1, the organization wanted to create work groups with specialized knowledge of products, vendors, and industries.
- A learner needs to gain experience-based knowledge from expert practitioners. In the sales organization example, sales representatives needed to gain experience by working with a seasoned colleague in order to compete against a well-entrenched competitor when selling a new product in a brand-new market segment.
- Learning needs of employees are individual and do not lend themselves to group interventions for skill development. For example, the diversity among the sales representatives in the sales organization example meant that different employees had unique skill development needs.
- An organization faces rapid changes and does not have enough time to capture, package, and disseminate tacit knowledge as it

becomes available. In the computer service organization example, some products changed monthly. As a result, the unique expertise developed in troubleshooting regarding those products could not be captured in a course or workshop and communicated to other team members. Cognitive apprenticeship arrangements enabled less experienced service professionals to listen in on the calls answered by experienced colleagues and to participate in a briefing session with the experienced colleagues when the call was closed.

Requirements

Successful implementation of a cognitive apprenticeship is dependent on some of the same conditions as mentoring:

- Management commitment. Managers must create the right climate and allocate needed resources.
- Selection of the right experts. Experts must not only be able to demonstrate excellence in their work but must also be willing and able to communicate well. (See table 7.2 for an example list of expert characteristics.)
- Learner commitment. As in mentoring, the learner must be committed to personal growth. (See table 6.2, page 63, for a list of learner characteristics.)
- Expert and learner orientation to establish expectations and to communicate techniques.

Table 7.2: Technical expert characteristics.

Attributes	Guiding Questions
Technical competence	Does the expert demonstrate effective technical skills?
Work knowledge	Does the expert demonstrate a grasp of the essentials of the work that the learner will be performing?
Willingness to help others	Is the expert committed to the growth and development of the learner?
Interpersonal skills	Does the expert effectively communicate with others?
Perceived status	Is the expert a well-respected member of the technical community?

- Clear definition of the skill development needs of the learner.
- Expert commitment in terms of time and the quality of his or her contribution to the engagement.
- A well-defined agreement. A list of mentoring and cognitive apprenticeship contract items appears in table 7.1.

The following requirements for successful implementation are unique to cognitive apprenticeships:

- Real-world projects and work situations exist that enable the learner to balance needed conceptual knowledge with reality-based experience.
- An accommodating work environment exists that enables the learner to observe an expert performer and enables the expert performer to observe the learner while practicing.

Design Guidelines

Coordinators, in conjunction with learners, perform tasks that ensure a successful cognitive apprenticeship at two levels—global and local.

Global tasks

Global tasks enable an organization to create a hospitable climate for implementing an effective cognitive apprenticeship. These tasks are similar to the ones described for mentoring:

- developing the necessary infrastructure
- allocating needed resources
- making necessary adjustments to the work environment
- providing required organizational support structure.

See chapter 6 for a more complete description of these tasks.

Local tasks

Coordinators and learners must perform a number of tasks at the local level to put a cognitive apprenticeship into operation. These tasks, like local tasks for a mentoring engagement, fall into four groups—planning, implementation, termination, and evaluation. (See figure 6.2 on page 64 for a depiction of the relationships among these four task groups.) See table 6.3, page 65, for a checklist of tasks performed in each group. The following is a short description of local tasks.

Planning tasks. The first group of tasks includes

- determining the skill development needs of the learner
- determining whether cognitive apprenticeships are an appropriate option
- selecting experts and matching them with apprentices
- defining a cognitive apprenticeship agreement by identifying the scope, activities, outcome, needed resources, timeline, and other requirements of the engagement. Table 7.1 shows the elements of such an agreement.

Implementation tasks. Orientation is a fundamental implementation task. The purpose of orientation is to help the expert and the learner to learn how cognitive apprenticeships are different from traditional teaching and learning techniques.

Cognitive apprenticeship activities are central to cognitive apprenticeships. A *cognitive apprenticeship* is an on-the-job learning partnership between an experienced practitioner and a less experienced individual. The purpose of the partnership is to help the learner develop the conceptual knowledge and cognitive strategies needed to solve problems, make decisions, and perform complex tasks.

Both the expert and the learner should actively participate in the creation of an effective cognitive apprenticeship opportunity. The expert is responsible for structuring the learning opportunities: selecting appropriate content, utilizing appropriate cognitive apprenticeship methods (for example, modeling, coaching), and sequencing learning activities. The learner actively participates in the engagement by identifying needed areas of skill development, using information provided by the expert, practicing skills and performing tasks under expert guidance, and evaluating his or her own progress. The following are the three tasks involved in the expert's structuring of a cognitive apprenticeship: (1) selecting appropriate content; (2) utilizing appropriate methods; and (3) sequencing learning activities.

1. **Selecting appropriate content.** Cognitive psychology research (Collins, et al., 1989; Collins, et al., 1991) shows that experts use at least four

types of knowledge to complete complex tasks—domain knowledge, heuristic knowledge, control strategies, and learning strategies.

- *Domain knowledge* includes facts, concepts, and procedures associated with a given profession (for example, law, information technology service, accounting, or instructional design). For instance, when a law student learns the four elements of a contract, he or she is gaining domain knowledge.

- *Heuristic knowledge* includes knowledge of effective techniques and approaches for accomplishing the required tasks. These techniques might be regarded as "tricks of the trade" or "rules of thumb." Most heuristic knowledge is experience based and is tacitly acquired by experts through the practice of solving many unstructured problems. For example, when a seasoned lawyer listens to a client's story for a few minutes and decides whether a contract existed or if it has been breached, the lawyer is using heuristic knowledge to decide the merits of a legal case.

- *Control strategies* involve the management of the problem-solving process. They are strategies that help an expert to set goals, select the most appropriate problem-solving strategy from among the various possible strategies, monitor implementation of the strategy, decide when to change strategies, and evaluate the outcome. For example, when a lawyer faces a complex contract dispute case, the lawyer searches his or her repertoire of heuristic knowledge about breach-of-contract cases and selects and adapts the most appropriate strategy for defending a client accused of breach of contract.

- *Learning strategies* include knowledge of how to learn. These strategies help people assess what they know and determine what they need to know. They also help them to determine how to explore new areas of knowledge, acquire new knowledge, and integrate the new knowledge with what they already know. Learners engaged in self-directed learning should use these strategies.

These four types of learning become apparent when an experienced lawyer encounters a new case. The lawyer applies rules and follows procedures to solve the case (for example, the four elements of a contract). When he or she encounters difficulty in solving the case, the lawyer uses control strategies to select from the list of heuristic strategies the one that best fits the situation. When applying the domain knowledge and the heuristic knowledge does not work, the experienced lawyer uses learning strategies to develop new understandings and to form new heuristic knowledge through experimentation and the seeking and gaining of new knowledge.

The expert in a cognitive apprenticeship engagement should ensure that the learner explores and acquires all four types of knowledge. See Collins, et al. (1991) for guidelines.

2. **Utilizing appropriate methods.** Collins, et al. (1989) recommend a number of methods to structure an effective cognitive apprenticeship. These methods provide the learner with the opportunity to observe, engage in, and discover strategies used by the expert in performing complex tasks.

Cognitive apprenticeship methods are *modeling, coaching, scaffolding, articulation, reflection,* and *exploration*. The first three methods (modeling, coaching, and scaffolding) help learners acquire knowledge through the process of observation and through guided and supported practice. Articulation and reflection help learners focus on their observation of the expert's strategies and gain conscious access to their own problem-solving strategies. Exploration encourages a learner's autonomy in identifying the problems to be solved. The following is a short description of each method. Readers are encouraged to see Collins, et al. (1989) and Collins, et al. (1991) for a more detailed description of these methods.

♦ *Modeling*. The expert provides the learner with an opportunity to observe the expert carrying out a task and develops a conceptual model of the processes required to complete the task. The expert must express his or her internal thought processes and activities to help the learner develop an understanding of the heuristic knowledge and control strategies. For example, when a junior partner in a law firm observes a senior partner interviewing a client to judge the merits of a legal case, the senior partner commentates while conducting the interview to identify his or her thought processes.

♦ *Coaching*. The expert observes the learner while he or she carries out a task and offers hints, feedback, reminders, and suggestions to bring the learner's performance level closer to that of the expert.

The expert should focus attention on the immediate and specific events or problems that arise as the learner attempts to carry out the target task. Experts can provide coaching either before, during, or after the learner performs the task. For example, a senior law partner observes the interaction between a junior lawyer and a client and provides prompts, hints, or feedback.

◆ *Scaffolding.* The expert provides support to help the learner carry out a task. This support is in the form of reminders and help. The expert should consider carrying out parts of the overall task that the learner cannot yet manage. Scaffolding involves a kind of cooperative problem-solving effort by the expert and learner. The intention is for the learner quickly to assume as much of the task as possible on his or her own. Once the learner has a grasp of the target skill, the expert should reduce or "fade" participation, by providing only limited hints, refinements, and feedback. For example, a junior lawyer initiates the client interview and gathers factual information about the case. The senior partner steps in to ask pointed questions during the interview session to generate and test hypotheses. The junior partner closes the interview. The portion of the client interview performed by the junior partner increases over time.

◆ *Articulation.* The expert helps the learner to articulate his or her knowledge, reasoning, or problem-solving processes as he or she carries out the task. Articulation helps bring newly learned knowledge to a high level of awareness and makes it accessible. For example, a senior law partner encourages a junior partner to commentate on his or her reasoning and thought processes while conducting client interviews. Furthermore, the junior partner summarizes the lessons learned during the interview and predicts how to apply them to future cases.

◆ *Reflection.* The expert helps the learner to compare his or her own problem-solving processes with those of the expert. Reflection aids self-evaluation. Reflection may include the use of various techniques (such as videotaping) for reproducing or replaying both the learner's and the expert's performances. Employees who use reflection during a cognitive apprenticeship engagement should continue to use it on the job to take advantage of this powerful, self-directed learning tool. For example, a junior law partner reflects on the patterns of reasoning and problem solving that he or she used during a client interview session and compares them to those used by a senior partner in earlier sessions. Audiotapes of the sessions or transcripts of the interviews might facilitate reflection.

◆ *Exploration.* The expert pushes the learner into a mode of problem solving on his or her own. If the expert wants the learner to learn how to frame questions and identify problems, he or she must encourage the learner to explore. For example, a senior law partner encourages a junior partner to dive into a case and start exploring different strategies for framing the case and devising a defense strategy to win the case.

3. **Sequencing learning activities.** In structuring an effective cognitive apprenticeship, the expert needs to be sensitive to the changing learning needs of the learner at different stages of skill acquisition. The expert can use three sequencing approaches: increasing complexity, increasing diversity, and presenting global skills before local skills.

◆ *Increasing complexity* involves constructing a sequence of steps for performing a complex task. Each step requires more skill and knowledge. In this way, the expert helps the learner progress from performing simple tasks to practicing tasks that require the integration and generalization of skills. For example, a senior law partner can expose a junior partner to complex cases gradually. As he or she gains more experience, the junior partner might start with simple cases first and gradually move on to more complex cases. For example, the junior partner starts with a simple contract case, in which a supplier has missed a delivery deadline, and later works on more complex cases involving several lawsuits and countersuits between two companies.

◆ *Increasing diversity* involves constructing a sequence of tasks that require an ever-widening variety of strategies or skills. As the learner applies skills to more diverse problem situations, he or she acquires a richer repertoire of strategies to use in unfamiliar situations. For example, a senior law partner gradually increases the junior partner's involvement in various activities in a case. The junior partner starts with interviewing the client and collecting factual information about the case and gradually becomes involved in other activities, such as devising a defense strategy, negotiating with the plaintiff's lawyers, or arguing a case in the courtroom.

◆ *Presenting global skills before local skills* gives a learner the opportunity to build a conceptual model of how subtasks fit together before attempting to perform all the subtasks. This approach sequences the learning activities so that the learner has a chance to apply the major skills involved in performing a complex task before being required to learn and remember all of the component skills. The main effect of this sequenced approach is to enable the learner to build a conceptual map of the problem-solving process before attending to the details of the terrain. For example, a junior partner learns about all major phases in a lawsuit—collecting background information, assessing the legal merits of a lawsuit, devising a defense strategy, and taking depositions—before spending time developing detailed skills in individual components (for example, comparing various defense strategies and tactics).

In addition, the learner collaborates with the expert in all of the learning activities. The learner performs the following specific tasks:

◆ *Researching.* The learner needs to play an active role in learning by following the leads provided by the expert and seeking, obtaining, analyzing, and synthesizing additional information.

◆ *Practicing.* The learner should seek opportunities to practice the newly gained skills and awareness under the expert's supervision.

◆ *Documenting engagement events.* Much of what the expert teaches the learner is not documented anywhere. The learner should take notes and prepare a personal log of the engagement.

Termination tasks. As a component of an effective learning environment, cognitive apprenticeships (like mentoring engagements) are well structured and bounded. The cognitive apprenticeship process is not open ended. The expert, the learner, and the coordinator monitor the learner's progress toward accomplishing the goals. Upon accomplishment of the cognitive apprenticeship goals, the engagement formally terminates.

Evaluation tasks. Evaluation is ongoing throughout the cognitive apprenticeship. Evaluation activities monitor the progress of a cognitive apprenticeship. The expert, the learner, and the coordinator each play a significant role in troubleshooting and improving the quality of the engagement. Midcourse corrections are sometimes needed to ensure the success of an apprenticeship. These interventions are based on problem areas. If the attempts at correction are not successful, all parties should be ready to terminate the engagement.

Evaluation tasks here are similar to those for mentoring. See table 6.5, page 68, for areas on which the learner, expert, and coordinator should focus to evaluate the success of the cognitive apprenticeship engagement.

Summary

A cognitive apprenticeship is a development technique that helps learners develop the cognitive skills required to perform complex tasks in contemporary organizations. It helps make tacit experience-based knowledge visible. Using this technique, expert practitioners help their colleagues develop problem-solving and decision-making skills in the context of their work. Like mentoring, cognitive apprenticeship is well structured and bounded, and is based on an agreement. As in the case of mentoring, cognitive apprenticeships work best when they are integrated with other components of an effective learning environment.

8

Internerships

Internships extend the learning opportunities beyond the boundaries of the immediate organization to include other organizations. By immersing learners in a new environment, internships enable learners to tap into the experiences and learning of others. The internship host may be another internal organization (such as a business unit, function, or field organization) or an external organization (such as a business partner, ally, or customer). Internships are a powerful learning method for an organization that is entering new market segments, offering new and more complex products and services, or entering new partnerships or alliances. In each of these cases, members of the organization need to develop complex skill sets at an accelerated pace, but the expertise to help develop these skills may not be available within the organization. Internships provide these organizations with an opportunity to explore the work environments of external groups as an enriched skill development setting. An internship can strengthen the relationship between the home organization and the host organization. The networking between professionals in both organizations provides continuing opportunities to share, learn, and enhance business. In addition, internships provide the host organization with a neutral feedback loop for assessing business practices based on the observations of independent observers (interns).

Consider the sales organization example cited in chapter 2. As a part of a new product introduction, the sales representatives needed to hone their consultative selling skills to position and sell complex solutions in a new market segment. The organization arranged an internship program with a customer organization that had been using consultative selling techniques to sell successfully in that market segment. The internship allowed a number of sales representatives to study the host organization's sales activities and practices closely, to interview people, to attend meetings, and to consider how they might adopt the experiences of those professionals. The sales representatives not only implemented the ideas obtained through the internship experience immediately upon their return, but also shared their knowledge with colleagues.

The experience of being in a different environment and constantly analyzing and reflecting on what makes another group or person successful is a powerful learning experience that can have a lasting impact on the individual. See table 8.1 for other internship examples.

Table 8.1: Examples of internships.

Learner	Environment	Internship Goal
Service product developer	Customer account	To develop an understanding of a customer's business needs, requirements, and market direction prior to upgrading the organization's service portfolio
Business development manager	Organization with a long history of successfully launching new products and services in a targeted market segment	To develop an understanding of the requirements, strategies, and capabilities necessary for new businesses
Service delivery professional	Product engineering group of a partner organization	To develop an understanding of serviceability requirements and strategies for a partner's product, prior to providing service for the product as part of a new alliance agreement
Operations manager	Best-in-class organization	To acquire knowledge of alternative business practices (for example, vendor management, purchasing, structuring a deal, designing a solution, and service delivery) to make operations in his or her home organization more efficient

Three roles exist in a successful internship engagement: a coordinator in the home organization, the intern, and a sponsor in the host organization. The coordinator's role is to set up the engagement, manage its progress, obtain needed resources, and evaluate it. The intern's role is to act as an investigator and observer. The sponsor's role is unique and crucial for the success of the internship. The sponsor is a knowledgeable and resourceful individual within the host organization who makes the internship experience effective. Table 8.2 shows the tasks performed by the coordinator, intern, and sponsor.

Table 8.2: Tasks performed by the coordinator, intern, and sponsor.

Roles	Tasks Performed
Coordinator	• Works with the intern to define his or her learning needs • Identifies an appropriate host organization • Works with the intern and host organization to define the engagement and participates in preparing the contract • Enlists management support and ensures allocation of needed resources • Monitors the progress of the internship engagement, troubleshoots potential problems, and applies midcourse correction to ensure a successful engagement • Orients the intern and the host and helps them understand their roles, expectations, and resources • Evaluates the success of the engagement and helps to terminate it at the appropriate time
Intern	• Identifies skill development needs and knowledge areas to explore in the host organization • Helps to define the scope, nature, and duration of the internship • Actively explores learning opportunities in the host organization • Observes, discusses, and validates perceptions; records findings and interpretations; and reflects on experiences • Monitors progress toward accomplishing the internship goals
Sponsor	• Participates in defining the internship experience for the intern and provides input to the internship agreement • Gives on-site support to the intern by being the primary contact, providing access to people and resources needed for the internship and resolving any issues and conflicts to improve the quality of the intern's experience • Evaluates the success of the engagement • Communicates and coordinates activities with the coordinator in the home organization to ensure the quality of the engagement

Criteria for Use

Like other development options (mentoring and cognitive apprenticeships), internships provide reality-based learning opportunities. They are appropriate when

- internal expertise in the organization to help employees develop the needed skills and knowledge is limited
- the organization is exploring new business opportunities and needs to build expertise in an accelerated manner
- a wealth of expertise exists in a domain in an external group or organization
- expertise in the host organization is not captured, organized, and made available in an easy-to-use format (for example, in books, reports, white papers, or best practices) and, as a result, an effective means to tap into expertise in the host organization is to have an intern explore the host organization to capture and learn about their best practices
- the professional already has valuable skills and needs only to build skills in a specific area.

Requirements

The success of an internship depends on the following factors:

- Management commitment, in both host and home organization, to sponsoring the internship and allocating needed resources to ensure its success.
- A set of criteria for identifying appropriate host organizations.
- High-level agreements with host organizations, which articulate conditions governing internships (for example, the number of interns per year, cost, provisions for safe-guarding proprietary information, and procedures for solving problems that might arise during the internship).
- Host organization commitment in terms of the time and the quality of the experience provided for the learner.

- A robust orientation and support program for the professionals during their internships. This program should consist of strategies for developing a purpose, exploring ideas, recording observations, analyzing findings, and reporting.

- A solid time commitment on the part of the home organization and the individual. Sometimes professionals or their managers think that they cannot afford time away from the job, but in some cases, an internship is the only viable alternative for providing the learner and the home organization with the required skills and know-how.

- Learner commitment. Like mentoring and cognitive apprenticeships, internships require the learner to demonstrate initiative and to approach the learning environment actively. See table 8.3 for a list of the necessary characteristics of an intern and questions to measure a prospective intern's commitment.

Table 8.3: Intern characteristics.

Attributes	Guiding Questions
Personal responsibility for learning	Is the learner committed to his or her learning and growth? Does the learner take initiative to learn? Does the learner have an inquiring mind?
Work habits	Is the intern capable of • dealing with complex work settings • dealing with ambiguity • working away from the support system of the home organization • staying on task and not being distracted by less relevant issues?
Background and organizational stature	Does the intern have the right background, level of experience, and organizational stature to represent the home organization and complete a successful internship? Has the intern prepared adequately for the internship? For example, has the learner done background research and established means for collecting, organizing, and reporting needed information?
Openness	Is the intern open to new ideas and nonjudgmental in dealing with unfamiliar experiences?
Interpersonal skills	Does the learner communicate effectively with others? Is the learner capable of analyzing, synthesizing, organizing, and communicating ideas effectively?

- Clear definition of the skill development needs of the learner.
- An internship agreement with the host organization that includes (1) expected learning outcomes, (2) needed resources and time commitments, (3) a termination process, and (4) provisions to handle confidential and proprietary information.
- An effective coordinator to plan the internship, establish expectations, contact and enlist the cooperation of host organizations, facilitate implementation, and evaluate the success of the internship.
- A supportive sponsor within the host organization to provide on-site support to the intern, solve problems, provide information and access to sources of information, and help with evaluating the success of the internship.

Design Guidelines

A successful internship, like a successful mentoring engagement or cognitive apprenticeship, requires that a series of tasks be performed by the intern, sponsor, coordinator, and managers in both the home and host organizations. These tasks exist at two levels: global and local.

Global tasks

Global level tasks enable an organization to create a hospitable climate for implementing an internship. These tasks include

- developing the necessary infrastructure
- allocating needed resources
- making necessary adjustments to the work environment, including making arrangements with the host organization to accept qualified candidates
- establishing a reward system.

Developing the necessary infrastructure. The following processes enable the creation of a successful internship engagement:

- Identifying desirable internal and external host group organizations. Table 8.4 shows a list of the attributes of hospitable host organizations.

Table 8.4: Attributes of a hospitable host organization.

Attributes	Guiding Questions
Needed expertise	Does the host organization provide an enriched learning ground for the intern to develop the desired skills and knowledge?
Openness and willingness to share	Does the host organization have a culture that enables the intern to explore ideas openly, observe, and engage in dialogue with peers?
Accommodating to unique needs of the intern	Is the host organization sensitive to the unique learning needs of the intern? Is it willing to make the necessary arrangements to ensure quality learning experiences for the intern?
Sponsor who is willing to help others	Is the host organization willing to appoint a resourceful sponsor who is willing to serve as a primary contact for the intern and actively create an effective internship experience for the learner?

- Defining and assessing skill development needs of the employees and selecting those skills that lend themselves to internships (see Criteria for Use).
- Matching learners' skill development needs with available host organizations.
- Developing an internship agreement between the learner, the coordinator in the home organization, and the sponsor in the host organization.
- Developing and implementing an orientation to prepare the learner to take advantage of the internship opportunity.

Allocating needed resources. Provisions should exist at the organizational level that provide the home organization with needed resources to successfully implement the internship engagement. In addition to the resources necessary for any development opportunity (mentoring, cognitive apprenticeship, or internship), the following resources are required for an internship:

- financial relief for the time that the intern spends in the host organization

- budget for living accommodation for the intern while staying away in the host organization
- budget for compensating the host organization for the cost associated with intern's stay in the host organization (office accommodation, telephone, computing resources).

Making necessary adjustments to the work environment. These arrangements include making contractual and operational agreements with the host organization to accommodate and reciprocate internship opportunities.

Establishing a reward system. A reward system will encourage employees and their managers to actively participate in and support internships. For example, managers who go the extra mile to arrange and manage an internship opportunity for their employees, and who make the necessary arrangements to carry on the work of the organization while the employee is away from work, should be rewarded for their activities and risk-taking behavior. The reward can be financial or it can be recognition by management and peers. Of course, employees who attend internship opportunities will be intrinsically rewarded by gaining new knowledge and establishing a professional network with their colleagues in other organizations. However, they also must be rewarded financially or recognized for taking the initiative to learn, for moving out of the comfort zone of their everyday jobs, and for allocating additional personal time to make the internship experience effective.

Local tasks

A number of tasks at a local level will successfully implement an internship opportunity. As in mentoring and cognitive apprenticeships, these tasks cluster into four groups: planning, implementation, termination, and evaluation. (See figure 6.2, page 64, for a depiction of the relationship among these four task groups.) Table 8.5 provides a checklist of tasks performed in each group. The following is a short description of local tasks.

Planning tasks. The first group of tasks enables you to do the following:

- Determine the skill development needs of the learner.
- Determine whether an internship is an appropriate option.

Table 8.5: Checklist of tasks performed at a local level to implement an internship.

Task Groups	(✓) Check Off Completed Tasks
Planning	**Determine skill development needs:** ❑ Define the skills needed to perform the job. ❑ Develop skill assessment tools. ❑ Assess individuals' skill development needs. ❑ Identify skill areas best suited for internships. **Select a host organization:** ❑ Define a set of criteria for selecting host organizations. ❑ Search for potential organizations that meet the criteria. ❑ Obtain information on potential host organizations. ❑ Match attributes of host organization with skill development needs of employees. ❑ Select the host organization. **Make arrangements with the host organization:** ❑ Identify a sponsor in the host organization. ❑ Identify the areas of focus for the internship. ❑ Work with the sponsor to determine the needed experiences, resources, and contacts for the intern. **Develop an internship agreement:** ❑ Define desired internship outcomes. ❑ Identify internship activities and experiences. ❑ Identify needed resources. ❑ Define timelines. ❑ Identify requirements (for example, provisions regarding handling proprietary information and special nondisclosure issues).
Implementing	**Orient intern and sponsor in the host organization:** ❑ Train intern and sponsor on the internship process. ❑ Help intern and sponsor understand their roles. ❑ Train intern on internship activities (for example, searching, reflecting, networking, validating perception, and offering feedback). **Implement internship agreement:** ❑ Resolve problems. ❑ Adapt engagement to emerging needs.
Terminating	❑ Monitor progress. ❑ Terminate the process upon accomplishment of the objectives.
Evaluating	❑ Evaluate how well the intern accomplished learning objectives. ❑ Evaluate appropriateness of the internship.

- Select a host organization and match its attributes with the skill development needs of the employee.
- Identify the areas of focus for the internship. To be successful, the internship should be focused and bounded and strike a balance between breadth and depth. That is, the internship should provide a broad perspective on the context of the host organization's experiences but provide an in-depth experience in only one or two areas for the learner.
- Formulate an agreement with the host organization by identifying the desired outcomes, scope, needed resources, timeline, and other requirements of the engagement. An internship agreement should state any unique requirements for this engagement, for example, provisions regarding handling proprietary information and special nondisclosure issues. Table 8.6 shows the elements of such an agreement.

Implementation tasks. The purpose of orientation is to help the intern and sponsor develop an understanding of their roles, expectations, and the requirements for a successful internship. The intern needs to learn efficient techniques such as searching for information, reflecting on experiences, actively seeking new experiences, networking within the host organization to establish collegial relationships, sharing learning, validating perception, and offering feedback with colleagues in the host organization.

Internship activities are tasks the intern performs in the host organization. An internship requires the learner to play an active and inquisitive role. The learner should collect, analyze, synthesize, and verify information within the host organization to gain an understanding in the targeted knowledge domains. The learner is expected to

- review and analyze plans, procedural documents, white papers, marketing collateral, and similar documents
- observe and record how sponsors perform tasks, how they make decisions, how they carry them out, and how they resolve conflicts
- volunteer to help practitioners in the host organization as they perform a variety of tasks
- engage in discussion with colleagues to gain a better understanding of the tacit knowledge involved in performing a variety of tasks

Table 8.6: Elements of an internship contract.

Elements	Guiding Questions
Expected performance outcome	What will the intern be able to do as a result of the engagement?
Areas of exploration	What questions or areas of exploration are the focus of this internship?
Activities	What activities will the intern perform in the host organization to gain experience?
Validation	How will the intern and sponsor in the host organization ensure the accuracy of the intern's observations?
Engagement evaluation	How will the effectiveness of the engagement be evaluated?
Resources	What resources (for example, budget and special tools) will the internship require?
Duration	What is the starting date and how long will the engagement last?
Frequency of meetings	How many times and how often will the intern meet with the sponsor?
Sponsor's time commitment	How many hours will the sponsor spend with the intern? How many hours will the sponsor spend participating in activities related to implementing the internship opportunity?
Intern's time commitment	How many hours will the intern spend at the host site to participate in activities related to the internship?
Provisions for working on customer project	What guidelines will govern the intern's participation in the host organization's customer projects?
Provisions for ensuring confidentiality of information	What steps will be taken to ensure confidentiality of the host organization's proprietary information?
Termination process	How will the engagement terminate? (For example, is a formal appraisal necessary? Should the sponsor and intern prepare a report?)
Signature	Have those involved (intern, sponsor, and other stakeholders) signed the contract?

- validate the accuracy of perceptions and observations with colleagues
- record and document understanding, perceptions, and heuristic knowledge to share with colleagues in the home organization upon return.

Termination. These tasks are intended to formally complete the internship engagement. Internships, like other components of an effective learning environment, are focused, well structured, and bounded. The sponsor and coordinator should monitor the learner's progress toward accomplishing the goals of the internship. The internship engagement should terminate when the learner has accomplished his or her objectives.

Evaluation. As in any development opportunity, evaluation is ongoing throughout the internship engagement. Evaluation is a joint activity among the learner, coordinator, and sponsor. See table 8.7 for areas of focus and questions to evaluate those areas.

Table 8.7: Areas of evaluation.

Areas of Focus	Guiding Questions
Intern and host organization match	• Was the host organization an appropriate learning ground for the intern's skill development needs? • Did the sponsor appropriately address the focus areas of the internship?
Commitment	Were the intern, sponsor, coordinator, and managers in both home and host organizations committed to the success of the engagement?
Orientation	Was the orientation adequate to help the learner and sponsor develop an understanding of their roles, responsibilities, and inquisitive learning techniques?
Resources	Were the allocated resources (for example, time, tools, and information) sufficient?
Internship activities	Was the engagement sufficiently flexible to optimize its meaningfulness and to enable the intern to take advantage of emergent opportunities?
Duration	Was the duration of the engagement appropriate for the intern's development objectives?

Integrating Internships with Other Development Opportunities

Internships extend learning opportunities beyond the boundaries of an organization. While the employee is at the host organization, he or she may take advantage of other resources within the host organization. For example, the coordinator could arrange a mentoring or cognitive apprenticeship engagement for the employee with experienced and expert employees in the host organization. Combining a mentoring engagement or cognitive apprenticeship in the context of an internship in the host organization can multiply the benefits of each opportunity. In the sales organization example cited in chapter 2, the sales representatives benefited from cognitive apprenticeship arrangements with experts in consultative selling at the host organization. The sales representatives met frequently with these experts and accompanied them on sales calls. The experts used cognitive apprenticeship techniques described in chapter 7 to help the learners to develop a profound understanding of consultative selling strategies.

Summary

Internships are a development technique intended to immerse the learner in an enriched learning environment. The experience of being in a different context and constantly analyzing and reflecting on what makes another group successful is a powerful learning experience that can have a lasting impact on the individual. Learners can immediately implement the ideas obtained through this experience upon returning to the home organization. They can also share their learning with their colleagues through the information- and experience-sharing component of the effective learning environment.

Part 3
Creating Effective Learning Environments

The process of creating an effective learning environment includes three interrelated clusters of activities. Figure 3 shows the flow of these three clusters of activities and their interrelationship.

Figure 3: Process for creating an effective learning environment.

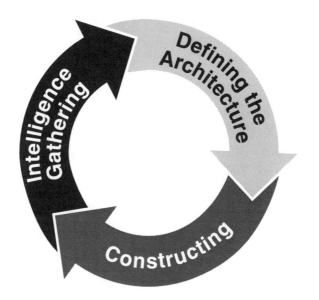

These activities are

- Intelligence gathering. These activities help to define the requirements for the learning environment and help to assess its effectiveness and business impact. Intelligence gathering includes both formal and informal data collection and analysis.

- Defining the architecture for the environment. These activities create a blueprint for the environment. They define and align the components of the environment and also integrate them into an architecture for a holistic, multifaceted learning environment.
- Constructing the environment. These activities put the architecture into operation. Instructional designers acquire specific options for formal learning, development, and information sharing and cultivate the environment.

Chapters 9, 10, and 11 describe each of these clusters of activities and provide guidelines for their successful completion.

An effective learning environment is not created in a vacuum, but in the larger context of workforce planning. Interrelated tasks must be completed to ensure its success. These tasks include

- defining business objectives
- defining needed capability (that is, required skills and knowledge to complete the work of the organization) and capacity (that is, the number of people with required skills) to achieve business objectives
- developing workforce plans at the organization level and at the work-group level
- orchestrating skill development efforts with other skill acquisition activities, such as hiring, contracting, or partnering with internal or external organizations.

These tasks must be completed prior to or in conjunction with the creation of an effective learning environment. A description of these tasks is beyond the scope of this book and the readers are encouraged to use related sources of more information.

9

Intelligence Gathering

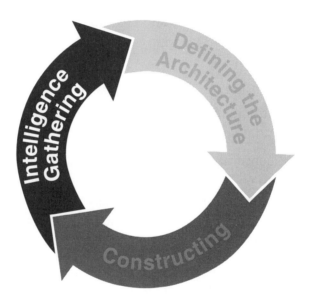

Figure 9.1: Process for creating an effective learning environment.

Intelligence gathering is not an event or a step in the process of creating the environment. It is an ongoing set of activities that starts early in the process and continues throughout the cycle of creating and implementing the environment, as well as in ongoing reevaluation, redesign, and improvement of the environment. Intelligence-gathering activities are similar to front-end analysis and formative and summative evaluation in conventional instructional development models.

Intelligence-gathering activities define the requirements for the effective learning environment. What business needs and learners' needs will the learning environment satisfy? What is the context and the specific work environment? What options for formal learning, information sharing, and development already exist, and what are their strengths and weaknesses? Once implemented, how effective is the learning environment? What is the impact of the learning environment on the business and on learners? How can the results of this evaluation be used to improve the learning environment?

Intelligence gathering consists of formal and informal data collection and analysis. Examples of informal activities include

- review and analysis of business strategies and reports
- review of operation reports and customer satisfaction survey reports
- tests of the accuracy of assumptions and decisions with the learners and business partners
- spontaneous dialogues with colleagues and learners
- review of learning and information products (to learn from them and/or to adopt and integrate them into the environment).

Formal intelligence gathering uses both qualitative and quantitative inquiry methods to collect and analyze data, make decisions based on the results, and report the results. These activities are based on the foundation of scientific inquiry and follow recommended quantitative and qualitative research design methods. Formal intelligence-gathering activities can be summarized in six steps:

1. Define the information needed to create the environment.
2. Formulate a data collection strategy and develop required plans.
3. Develop and test data-gathering instruments and procedures.
4. Collect the needed data.
5. Analyze the data and communicate the results.
6. Formulate a course of action.

The remainder of this chapter examines each step more closely. Detailed guidelines for performing these tasks are beyond the scope of this book. Readers are encouraged to review books on qualitative, quantitative, and evaluation design methods (for example, Fink and Kosecoff, 1985; Rossett, 1987; McMillan and Schumacher, 1993).

1. Define the Needed Information

The instructional designer must define clearly the types of information needed to create a learning environment and to evaluate its effectiveness. He or she can gather the information needed to create an effective learning environment by finding answers to the following questions:

- What are the business requirements?
- What should the workforce know or be able to do to meet the business requirements?
- What kind of requirements does the work environment impose on the learning environment?
- What sort of infrastructure and resources are required in the organization itself, and which are already available?
- What learning, information, and development solutions already exist?
- Once a learning environment has been implemented, how effective is it? What is the business impact?

Table 9.1 shows types of needed information and their possible use and sources.

What are the business, performance, and skill requirements?

Organizations, like living organisms, are influenced by their environments. The environment constantly imposes new challenges and provides new opportunities. Organizations must redefine and fine-tune their business objectives and strategies continuously. These new objectives and associated strategies impose new performance requirements on employees. In the sales organization example cited earlier, the company formulated a business strategy to offset declining revenue from a shrinking market segment. This strategy was to enter a new market segment by introducing a new product and gain a ten percent increase in revenue from that segment. This new strategy imposed new performance requirements on the sales force. They were asked to achieve at least 20 percent of their sales quota in the new market segment.

The creation of a learning environment that is responsive to the business needs of an organization requires the continuous collection of information

Table 9.1: Information needed to create and evaluate an effective learning environment.

Types of Information	Possible Use	Potential Source
What are the requirements? • Business • Workforce • Work environment What are the dependencies? • Infrastructure • Resources	Define an environment that meets a variety of requirements and will be successfully implemented	• Documents—strategic plans, long-range plans, operation plans, white papers, industry and market reports • Managers—business, human resources, line management • Product and service engineering groups • Learners
What is available? • Resources • Infrastructure • Existing learning, development, and information-sharing options	• Audit current capabilities to determine the scope of needed modification • Integrate the current options into the environment • Learn from existing solutions and best practices to enhance chances of success	• Current learning and development processes, practices, and infrastructure • Current and budgeted resources for learning and development
How effective is the learning environment and what is its business impact?	• Determine the effectiveness of an environment and make the necessary improvement • Assess the business impact of implementing an environment	• Customer feedback • Learner performance on the job • Business indicators

on business objectives, strategy, and requirements and the use of this information to define performance and skill requirements. Table 9.2 shows the interrelationships among business, performance, skills, and knowledge requirements.

Once an organization understands its business needs and performance requirements, it can determine its workforce requirements. Continuing with the earlier example, what types of skills and knowledge does the sales force need to be able to penetrate the new market segment and achieve 20 percent of their sales quota in that segment? The skills definition project conducted in the sales organization revealed that the sales force needed skills and knowledge in the following areas:

- knowledge of the dynamics of the new market segment (including competition)
- ability to use a consultative selling technique
- knowledge of the new product
- ability to sell the new product in the new market segment using an unfamiliar selling technique.

In addition to defining the needed skills and knowledge, the architect of the learning environment must gain an understanding of the current skill set of the workforce. Analysis of the gap between the needed and current skill set is extremely important in creating a learning environment that addresses skill deficiencies in a prioritized manner. The changing nature of business and of associated skill sets makes the continuous gathering of new intelligence important.

An understanding of the business context, objectives, and strategies, as well as the associated requirements that are imposed on the employees, is crucial to the success of a learning environment. In the above example, the challenge for the organization was to determine the most effective means to acquire the needed skills and knowledge. Such an understanding of the business requirements (gained through intelligence-gathering activities)

Table 9.2: Interrelationship among business, performance, and skill requirements (sales organization example).

Objective, Strategy, and Requirements	Description
Business objectives	To offset declining revenue in a shrinking market segment
Business strategy	To introduce a new product in a new market segment
Business requirements	To penetrate a new market segment and gain 10 percent market share
Sales force performance requirements	To achieve 20 percent of sales quota in the new market segment by selling the new product
Skill and knowledge requirements	• Knowledge of dynamics of the new market segment • Ability to use new selling technique (consultative selling) • Knowledge of the new product • Ability to sell the new product in the new market segment using a new selling technique (that is, consultative selling)

enabled the organization to create learning opportunities that were responsive to changing business needs.

What are the work environment requirements?

The work environment influences an effective learning environment, just as the learning environment shapes the work environment in the long term. Learning opportunities in an effective learning environment are well integrated with work. For example, in cognitive apprenticeships the learners observe the experts as they perform work. The expert also observes the apprentice as he or she performs portions of the work in the real-world situations. Creating a successful cognitive apprenticeship opportunity requires an in-depth understanding of the work environment and the constraints that it imposes on learning activities. In the sales example, the experience- and information-sharing component of the learning environment was conducive to the work environment of the sales force. For example, a monthly conference call maximized the sales representatives' ability to take advantage of new product experience–sharing sessions and took the place of face-to-face meetings. This decision was based on the fact that the sales force was distributed throughout the world.

Work environment information is crucial to achieving two goals: (1) defining requirements that the work environment imposes on the learning environment; (2) defining requirements for changing the work environment to accommodate the learning environment.

As is the case with any other organizational intervention, deployment of an effective learning environment creates a disequilibrium in the work environment. In the short run, the learning environment should fit harmoniously into the work environment. A proper match between learning opportunities and the constraints of the work environment makes the opportunities more useful and speeds their acceptance. In the long run, once the learning environment is accepted and its usefulness proven, the work environment should change to accommodate and facilitate the learning environment. To increase the effectiveness and efficiency of cognitive apprenticeship learning opportunities, an organization might, for example, change its project planning and management practices to provide more opportunities for pairing junior and senior employees in the context of real-world projects.

What infrastructure and resources are required?

Certain conditions should exist in the environment to enable successful implementation of a learning environment. Examples of these conditions, or dependencies, are the infrastructure, resources, and reward structure. Infrastructure refers to the tools, processes, procedures, and practices needed to implement the environment effectively. See chapter 11 for a detailed discussion of the infrastructure requirement for different components of an effective learning environment. Resources include the time, funding, and people needed to make a learning environment happen and to sustain it over time. Successful implementation of an effective learning environment requires a robust reward system that will encourage initiative from learners, commitment from management, and support from colleagues. Some examples of reward systems follow:

- The organization should recognize business managers for actively participating in successful implementation of the learning environment.
- The organization should reward experienced colleagues and expert performers for actively participating in mentoring and cognitive apprenticeship opportunities. These employees spend quality time helping their colleagues develop and maintain the required skill set.
- The organization should recognize and reward employees for continuously learning new skills in support of the strategic directions of the organization.

An audit of the current infrastructure, resources, and reward system can determine the scope of needed modification.

What learning, information, and development solutions already exist?

A review of existing learning and information solutions makes it possible to identify the following:

- Solutions that are appropriate to be adopted "as is" in the learning environment. For example, existing internal and external courses (both lecture and self-paced learning modules) that meet skill development requirements can be adopted in the formal learning component of the environment.

- Innovations in other solutions that can be copied when developing solutions. For example, a review of best practices in sharing experience and information (such as, intranet-based video conferencing) can generate ideas for creating effective information-sharing opportunities in the organization.

Such a review should be ongoing. Many sources contain information about existing learning solutions. Examples of these sources are university and vendor catalogs, Web sites, exhibitions in professional organizations, the practices of market leaders, benchmarking and best practices meetings with colleagues, and commercially available learning solutions.

A review of existing learning solutions should always include existing solutions inside the organization. Many solutions may exist in an organization that it can adopt and integrate into an effective learning environment. Reuse of solutions and the associated savings in learning from existing solutions and best practices improve the likelihood of a successful learning environment.

How effective is the learning environment? What is the business impact?

To determine the business impact of an effective learning environment and to demonstrate its added value, an organization should identify and monitor performance indicators (for example, sales quotas) and business indicators (for example, revenue). A combination of formal evaluation techniques, such as Kirkpatrick's 1996 model, and informal intelligence-gathering techniques, such as anecdotal evidence and testimonials from business managers and employees, is most effective. Organizations facing tight resources and competing priorities need to evaluate their investment choices continuously. Intelligence-gathering activities must constantly monitor business and performance indicators and link them to the impact of a learning environment to prove its effectiveness and to build a business case for continuous investment in learning in times of competing priorities. For example, the group of sales representatives in the sales organization needed to develop skills in consultative selling and improve their ability to sell a complex product to a new market segment. As a part of establishing internship and cognitive apprenticeship opportunities, instructional designers collected sales performance data (that is, sales quota and market share) for participants in the learning environment and reported to the management team. In addition, they conducted interviews with the sales representatives and their managers several times to collect anecdotal information on the effectiveness of the learning environment.

2. Formulate a Data Collection Strategy and Develop Required Plans

The next step after defining the needed information is devising a data collection and analysis strategy. This strategy should identify the sources of information, determine sampling techniques, select data collection instruments, determine data collection and analysis techniques, define timelines, and determine needed resources. See table 9.3 for a list of questions that the strategy should answer.

Table 9.3: Data collection and analysis questions.

Area	Questions
Data sources	• What are the primary and secondary sources of information?
Procedures	• What are the best ways to tap into sources of information? • What are the best procedures for collecting data?
Sampling	• What is the sampling method? • What is the sample size?
Instrumentation	• What are the best instruments for collecting data? • How will the instruments be administered? • How will the instruments be piloted?
Data analysis	• How will the data be analyzed? • How will the data be cross-validated?
Needed resources	• What are the needed data collection and analysis resources?
Timeline	• What is the data collection and analysis schedule?

A plan should articulate the formal data collection and analysis strategy, identifying all needed resources and including timelines. See Rossett (1987) for more detail on developing a plan for data collection and analysis.

Data sources

Data can be collected not only from people but also from measurement of performance indicators. Information on business requirements can be obtained from strategic and operational documents, including white papers and industry and market reports. Business managers, human resource managers, and line managers can provide essential information on workforce requirements, the work environment, the infrastructure, and resource dependencies. Product and service engineering groups can help to define workforce needs, as can members of the workforce themselves.

Data is not collected only once. An effective learning environment requires continuous input and feedback from a variety of constituencies— learners, line managers, business managers, mentors, coordinators, and host organizations. Frequent and ongoing feedback should be obtained from these stakeholders, both to design an effective learning environment and to improve it. Data should be continuously collected and the environment constantly upgraded.

The list of data sources should be kept flexible. Some sources are identified prior to data collection, whereas others are identified during data collection for follow-up or validation of collected data.

Sampling

A sampling technique defines how many people to interview and whom to interview, or how to select a representative number of performance indicators. Tapping into every source of information (for example, interviewing all line managers and every potential learner or examining every report) is impossible. A representative sample of data sources can provide the needed data. Several sampling techniques exist that ensure a representative sample. One can generalize findings from a good sample and make decisions based on those findings. A description of sampling techniques is beyond the scope of this book. Proper sampling is extremely important, however, and readers are encouraged to review relevant references (Fink and Kosecoff, 1985; McMillan and Schumacher, 1993).

3. Develop and Test Data-Gathering Instruments and Procedures

A variety of data collection tools are available. Table 9.4 provides a list of tools and their advantages and disadvantages.

Answers to the following questions can help determine the best tool:

- What is the purpose of data collection? For example, is the purpose to define requirements for the learning environment, to receive feedback from learners to revise a component of the environment, or to assess the business impact of the environment?

- Is the tool appropriate for data source? For example, an interview is appropriate for data sources such as expert performers and subject matter experts. A focus group is more appropriate for gaining input from customers and clients. Tests are appropriate tools for gaining objective information on the effectiveness of a learning module.

- What are advantages and limitations of the tool?

- Are the needed resources available to use the tool? For example, is there a need for an interviewer, or for tools to record observations, or for software to collect and analyze detailed information from performance indicators?

- What is the organization's past experience and acceptance of a tool? For example, has there been a disruption caused by observing learners in the work environment, by administering a test, or by administering long questionnaires?

- What is the preference and expertise of the people who use the tool?

Table 9.4: Comparison of data collection tools.

Tools	Advantages	Disadvantages
Questionnaire	Provides access to a large number of people	Not suited for gaining in-depth, "rich" information
Interview	Provides in-depth, "rich" information	Labor intensive
Observation	Provides reality-based and objective information	Not always feasible
Existing data, documents, records, work samples	Provide objective, detailed information	Not always available or accessible
Focus groups	Provide multiple perspectives and an opportunity to validate collected information	Focus group members might influence what others say
Tests	Provide objective information	Tests might intimidate the audience and therefore not be valid

For more detailed information on data collection tools, see Fink and Kosecoff (1985) and Rossett (1987).

4. Collect the Needed Information

The data collection strategy is implemented during this stage. Depending on the design method (qualitative or quantitative), different tasks need to be performed to ensure the integrity and accuracy of collected data. See McMillan and Schumacher (1993) for guidelines on data collection.

5. Analyze the Data and Communicate the Results

Data analysis comprises three tasks:

- organizing and summarizing the data
- interpreting the data
- making decisions based on findings or making recommendations based on the data interpretation.

The selected research design and method (quantitative, qualitative, or evaluative) should determine the appropriate methods for organizing, summarizing, and interpreting the data. See McMillan and Schumacher (1993) for more detail.

The results of data analysis should provide information in the following areas:

- Business requirements. Business requirements include business objectives, strategies, and operational priorities.
- Performance requirements for individuals and groups. These requirements are derived from business needs and objectives. An example of a performance requirement is an increase in the sales quota for an organization's sales force from 10 to 20 percent in a market segment to meet a market share expansion objective.
- Workforce requirements. These requirements are the skills and knowledge needed by employees to meet performance requirements imposed by business needs.

- Infrastructure and resources. The data should provide a list of resources (time, funds, and people) and infrastructure (tools, processes, and procedures) needed to implement the learning environment successfully, as well as a list of available resources and a description of an infrastructure that can be adopted.

- Existing learning solutions. The data should list the available formal learning, information-sharing, and development opportunities that the organization can adopt and integrate into the environment. Evaluation data on their appropriateness and effectiveness also should be compiled.

- Effectiveness and business impact of the learning environment. During rapid prototyping and implementation of the environment, additional information becomes available. This information includes feedback from learners and other stakeholders and performance and business indicators. It can confirm the effectiveness and appropriateness of the learning environment and its components. The organization can use the feedback to revise and fine-tune the environment continuously.

6. Formulate a Course of Action

The insight gained during the data collection and analysis phases can lead to a variety of decisions. The decisions and resulting actions fall into four categories:

- Defining the architecture for the environment. Decisions about the architecture of the environment are based on requirements defined during intelligence gathering.

- Acquiring and developing components of the environment and integrating them into the environment. The insight gained from the requirements and existing learning solutions help make decisions about using and integrating existing solutions or developing or acquiring new components for the environment. Chapter 11 describes activities based on these decisions.

- Modifying and continuously improving the learning environment and its components. These decisions are based on the input received from learners and other stakeholders.

- Articulating the added value of the learning environment and ensuring continuous support for it. These decisions and recommendations are made based on the information gained from assessing the effectiveness and business impact of the environment.

Summary

Intelligence-gathering activities provide insight into the creation and continuous improvement of an effective learning environment. Intelligence gathering is an ongoing activity, consisting of both formal and informal efforts. Creators, users, and sponsors of a learning environment continuously gather, analyze, and interpret a variety of information from various sources. The activities range from a spontaneous conversation with a learner in a hallway to the administration of a multiple-page skill assessment survey to a worldwide audience. Requirements for an effective learning environment derive from business and learner needs and the unique attributes of the work environment. They represent conditions that the learning environment should meet to be effective and to add value to the organization. The organization should define business, workforce, and work environment requirements early in the process of creating the environment and continuously update it. Dependencies are conditions that must exist in the wider environment to enable a successful implementation of the learning environment. Examples of dependencies are needed infrastructure and resources. Continuous intelligence gathering in the areas of infrastructure, resources, and available and evolving learning and information solutions is a major success factor in implementing an effective learning environment. An effective learning environment responds to the changing skill development needs of an organization and, as a result, should truly reflect the requirements of business, members of the workforce, and the work environment. The creation and maintenance of an effective learning environment in a dynamic organization requires an inquiring mind and a passion for making decisions based on accurate and up-to-date information. Table 9.5 provides a checklist to guide intelligence-gathering activities.

Table 9.5: Checklist of intelligence-gathering activities.

Activity Clusters	(✓)	Actions
Define the needed information	❑ ❑ ❑ ❑	Define business, skills, and work environment Define infrastructure and resource requirements Identify existing learning, information, and development solutions Determine the effectiveness and business impact of the learning environment
Formulate a data collection strategy and develop required plans	❑ ❑ ❑ ❑ ❑	Identify sources of information Determine sampling techniques Select data collection instruments Determine data collection and analysis techniques Define timelines and determine needed resources
Develop and test data-gathering instruments and procedures	❑ ❑ ❑ ❑ ❑ ❑	Determine the purpose of data collection (for example, defining requirements, receiving feedback, and assessing effectiveness) Identify advantages and limitations of selected data collection tools and procedures Construct the instruments (for example, create questionnaire, develop interview protocol, or construct test) Define data collection procedures Pilot the instrument and data collection procedures Develop instructions for collecting data
Collect the needed data	❑ ❑	Follow the data collection procedure (for example, administer tests and questionnaires, conduct interviews, and facilitate focus groups) Ensure integrity and accuracy of data collection activities
Analyze the data and communicate the results	❑ ❑ ❑ ❑ ❑	Review, organize, and summarize data Use appropriate statistical analysis procedures for quantitative data Interpret the data Define requirements, needed infrastructure, existing resources and learning solutions, and revisions and upgrades to the learning environment Write reports and prepare presentations
Formulate a course of action	❑ ❑ ❑ ❑	Make decisions regarding architecture of the environment acquisition or development of components of the environment modification and continuous improvement of the environment added value of the environment

Defining the Environment Architecture

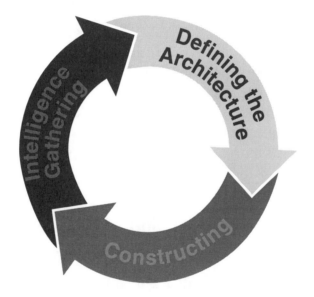

Figure 10.1: Process for creating an effective learning environment.

The learning environment architecture is an abstraction that can guide the creation of the environment. Just as a building architect, based on the client's expectations and resources, determines the dimensions of a house, the number of rooms, the hallways and stairs that connect the rooms, the placement of plumbing and heating components, and other details, the architect of an effective learning environment determines the structure of the environment based on information collected about the organization's needs and resources.

The architecture is based on the business requirements, skill development needs, and work environment requirements defined during intelligence-gathering efforts. The architecture

- defines components of the environment (opportunities for formal learning, information and experience sharing, and development)
- describes the interrelationships among the components and demonstrates how the components fit into a whole system
- describes the conditions required to implement the environment successfully
- provides a framework and a set of guidelines for selecting, developing, and orchestrating components of the environment.

The architect does not, however, specify in detail the content, media, and methods for formal learning options. Instead, he or she defines the desirable learning outcomes of the formal learning options and provides broad guidelines for obtaining, customizing, or developing formal learning options. The architecture gives an organization the flexibility to upgrade the learning environment continuously by plugging in new courses and learning products as they become available.

Process for Defining an Architecture

The process of defining an architecture for an effective learning environment includes the six steps outlined in table 10.1.

The following is a short description of these steps.

1. **Analyze the requirements.** Requirements are identified during the intelligence-gathering phase, and analysis of those requirements is ongoing. An effective learning environment should respond to requirements from three perspectives: the business, the learner, and the work environment. An architect should perform the following three complementary activities:

   ◆ Strive to develop a profound understanding of business objectives, strategies, issues, and controlling factors. The business landscape is constantly changing, and the architect must continuously update information.

◆ Analyze the tasks performed by employees to meet the business objectives and further define the skills and knowledge needed to perform the tasks. Defining the needed skills is a prerequisite for defining an effective learning environment.

◆ Strive to understand the work environment. The learning environment is a subsystem within the larger system of the work environment. In order to fit the learning environment harmoniously into the work environment, the architect must thoroughly understand the requirements that the work environment imposes on an effective learning environment. See table 9.2, page 105, for examples of different types of requirements that guided the development of a learning environment for the sales organization example.

Table 10.1: Steps for creating an architecture.

Steps	Description
1	Analyze the requirements for the environment.
2	Decide which learning opportunities (that is, formal learning, information sharing, or development) best meet the skill development needs of the employees.
3	Define components.
4	Describe the interrelationships among components.
5	Identify conditions (resources, infrastructure, and reward system) needed to implement the environment successfully.
6	Develop guidelines for implementing the environment (guidelines for identifying skill development needs of employees, for selecting learning opportunities, and for obtaining approval and allocating needed resources).

2. **Decide which learning opportunities (that is, formal learning, information sharing, and development) best meet the skill development needs of the employees.** Part 2 of this book discusses the criteria for selection of formal learning, experience-sharing, and development options. Table 10.2 shows an example of proposed learning options for a select number of skills needed by the computer help-desk service professionals described in chapter 1. When more than one skill development option is listed, the number indicates

Table 10.2: Proposed learning options for a sample of professional skills.

Skill/Knowledge	Learning Options
Negotiation	
Presenting options and obtaining agreement	Mentoring
Creating and developing win/win scenarios	Mentoring
Assessing the opportunities of a situation	Mentoring
Prioritizing objectives	Mentoring
Using conflict resolution techniques (compromising, venting anger constructively)	1. Cognitive apprenticeship 2. Mentoring
Problem solving	
Knowledge of problem escalation procedures and protocol	1. Mentoring 2. Formal learning
Recognizing potential problems	Cognitive apprenticeship
Analyzing problems from multiple perspectives	1. Cognitive apprenticeship 2. Mentoring
Identifying and enlisting appropriate resources (experts) to help resolve problems	Mentoring
Using problem-solving techniques (brainstorming, prioritizing, value clarification)	Cognitive apprenticeship
Project management	
Applying standard project management methodologies	Formal learning
Planning, monitoring, and controlling project processes	Cognitive apprenticeship
Assessing and managing risk	Cognitive apprenticeship
Forecasting, tracking, and controlling project budgets	Cognitive apprenticeship
Identifying, allocating, and managing project team resources based on project requirements	Cognitive apprenticeship
Using standard project management tools (MS Project)	Cognitive apprenticeship
Account management	
Orienting customers to the benefits of the organization's portfolio and business initiatives	1. Mentoring 2. Formal learning 3. Information sharing
Understanding the customer's business and needs (industry/market, computing environment)	1. Cognitive apprenticeship 2. Internship
Building and maintaining long-term customer relationships	Mentoring

whether that option is a primary option or a supporting option used for reinforcement or as an alternative.

3. Define components of the environment:

◆ Formal learning. For each formal learning opportunity, the architect must define learning objectives, determine the scope and sequence of the content, and propose appropriate media and methods. Recommendations on media and methods should not limit the flexibility of the organization in taking advantage of existing and new courses and learning modules. Table 10.3 shows an example of the definition of one formal learning module to teach the sales force the features, function, and competitive positioning of a new product.

Table 10.3: An example of a learning module.

Title: Competitive positioning of the new product

Length: Half day

Goals: Sales representatives should be able to

- demonstrate an in-depth knowledge of the functions and features of the new product
- demonstrate an understanding of the types of customer problems that the new product is intended to solve
- demonstrate a knowledge of competitive products in the market place
- position the product against competitive products and articulate its added value.

Learning strategy: To accomplish the learning goals a two-component strategy is recommended:

- a combination of lecture and demonstration of basic features of the product and competitive products
- a simulation to exercise matching product features with customer problems and positioning the product against competition.

◆ Information and experience sharing. The architect should describe selected information- and experience-sharing options in detail. For example, if the monthly conference call meetings and notes conference have been identified, the needed infrastructure and resources for their successful implementation should now be described. To illustrate, enough telephone lines must be available for the conference call to enable the sales force to call in. For the notes conference, specific computer and networking capabilities are needed to facilitate effective and efficient information exchange. Information- and experience-sharing options should take advantage of the current infrastructure and should be consistent with the organization's culture and common practices.

◆ Development options (cognitive apprenticeships, mentoring, and internships). The architect should provide a detailed description of development options. For example, after selecting a combination of internships and cognitive apprenticeships for the sales force, then the architect must define a process for assigning each sales representative to an expert in the host organization. He or she must describe the nature of the relationship and the specific responsibilities and expectations for each participant. Chapters 6, 7, and 8 provide detailed guidelines for selecting, defining, and implementing development options.

4. **Describe the interrelationships among components.** Different learning components complement each other. All three categories of learning and development options should operate as a system. Formal learning components are usually intended to help learners develop foundation skills. Development opportunities help learners to increase their proficiency after gaining the foundation skills. The architect should define and map the relationships among the learning and development options to provide a road map for the learners. For example, consultative selling skills, as described in the sales organization example, might be developed first through a course, sharpened through a cognitive apprenticeship, and fine-tuned through a sharing of information and experience with fellow sales representatives.

5. **Identify conditions (resources, infrastructure, and reward system) needed to implement the environment successfully.** For example, the organization must invest in obtaining, storing, and making the formal learning options available. An infrastructure is necessary to the implementation of options for sharing infor-mation and experience. Changes in the reward structure may encourage participation in cognitive apprenticeships and other development options.

6. **Develop guidelines for implementing the environment.** The architect should define a set of guidelines for implementing the learning environment and its components. Guidelines should cover the following areas:

- Identifying skill development needs of the learners. The architect should provide clear guidelines about how to determine skill development needs of the learners. For example, the architect might develop a self-assessment tool and set guidelines for administration and interpretation of the tool. Other ways to determine skill development needs of learners include self-assessment tools, tests, observation, and informal reports by colleagues, customers, and managers.

- Selecting specific options for formal learning, information sharing, and development. These guidelines help learners and their managers select appropriate learning options.

- Organizing the selected skill development activities into a learning and development plan for the learners.

- Obtaining approval and allocating needed resources to implement the learning and development plan.

The following example illustrates the process used to define an architecture for an effective learning environment. As part of a reengineering effort, a software development organization decided to institutionalize a new product "requirement management" (RM) process. The organization created the new process based on best practices in the field of software engineering by four internal RM experts. The process consisted of a set of tools and practices for defining, prioritizing, tracking, and managing requirements for new products. To ensure successful implementation of the new process, the organization decided to hire 18 RM consultants. The plan was to train the newly hired consultants in the new RM process and to assign them to the product development teams. Their role was to

- facilitate implementation of the new RM process
- help the product development team develop skills in implementing the new RM process.

To ensure that the newly hired consultants had the right skill set, an instructional designer collaborated with the designers of the new RM process to define the tasks performed by RM consultants and the skills and knowledge needed to perform the tasks. Together, they identified eight clusters of tasks. See table 10.4 for a list of these clusters. Each cluster contained between four and 11 subtasks. Table 10.5 shows a list of tasks within in a single cluster: "Voice of Customer" data gathering.

Table 10.4: Requirement management task clusters.

Task Clusters
• Client engagement and team enrollment • Formation setup • "Voice of Customer" data gathering • Analysis of "Voice of Customer" • Competitive analysis • Change management • Ongoing support • Managing the process

Table 10.5: Tasks within "Voice of Customer" data-gathering cluster.

Tasks
• Encourage the team to gather as much peripheral information on their "product" as possible. • Select appropriate methods for direct customer engagement (for example, surveys, contextual inquiry, focus group, prototype). • Help the team to learn the Contextual Inquiry (CI) interview technique/process through formal presentations, practice sessions, and coaching. • Plan CI in detail. • Help the team to develop the CI focus and "script" for the customer visits. • Lead the complete team through the analysis of the "Voice of Customer" data (CI visit information, industry reports, survey results) and help them organize the information into a hierarchy (affinity diagram).

The team identified seven skill and knowledge clusters as crucial for performing requirement management tasks. Table 10.6 displays these clusters. Each cluster contained between four and twelve skill and knowledge areas. Table 10.7 shows a list of the skill and knowledge areas for one of the clusters: techniques knowledge.

The team divided the required skills and knowledge into two groups: skills brought to the job and skills developed on the job through learning and development activities. Skills brought to the job were generic-consulting and group facilitation skills, such as communication skills, problem-resolution skills, knowledge of group dynamics, ability to deal with ambiguity, conflict resolution skills, and leadership skills. These skills were used to screen the candidates.

Table 10.6: Requirement management skill clusters.

Skill and Knowledge Clusters
• Context knowledge • RM process knowledge • Techniques knowledge • Data-collection and analysis ability • Team and meeting facilitation ability • Communication • Mentoring and teaching

Table 10.7: Skills and knowledge within requirement management techniques knowledge cluster.

Skill and Knowledge Areas
• In-depth knowledge of "Voice of Customer" techniques (for example, CI, Quality Function Deployment) • Ability to recognize when the use of these techniques is appropriate • Ability to implement the techniques in a variety of situations • Ability to explain the techniques in simple terms and create an environment in which team members can learn about the techniques in a just-in-time manner • Knowledge of configuration management • Knowledge of revision control techniques • Ability to do cost-benefit analysis • Knowledge of project-planning practices • Ability to manage projects

To preserve the integrity of the new RM process, the newly hired RM consultants needed to develop a set of complex skills and gain immediate access to new information that was becoming available through practice. More specifically, they needed to

- become socialized to the context of the new organization, product engineering process, and practices
- gain basic knowledge about the RM process, tools, and techniques
- develop an in-depth understanding of the appropriate use of RM techniques in various project conditions

- access their colleagues' experience-based knowledge and information quickly and continuously.

Conventional training techniques, such as a series of courses or unstructured mentoring, were not conducive to the needs of the organization. To meet the development needs of the newly hired RM consultants, the organization decided to create an effective learning environment. The architect used the following steps for defining an architecture.

1. **Analyze the requirements.** Through a series of dialogues with the designers of the new RM process and business managers, the learning environment architect

   - gained a profound understanding of the business objectives and strategies of the organization
   - reviewed the tasks performed by the RM consultants and the required skills to perform the tasks
   - gained an understanding of the work environment and conditions under which the RM managers complete their work.

2. **Determine the most appropriate learning opportunities.** The learning environment architecture team matched the skill requirement needs of the group with possible learning and development alternatives and decided to provide the following:

   - a set of formal learning opportunities to help RM consultants gain basic knowledge about the RM process, tools, and techniques, and related professional skills (for example, team formation)
   - mentoring opportunities to help RM consultants become socialized to the context of the new organization, product engineering processes, and practices
   - cognitive apprenticeship opportunities to help RM consultants develop an in-depth understanding of the appropriate use of RM techniques in various project conditions
   - biweekly meetings and a notes conference moderated by expert RM consultants to help RM consultants access their colleagues' experience-based knowledge and information.

3. **Define components.** The formal learning component of the environment covered the nine skill and knowledge areas listed in table 10.8.

Table 10.8: Skill and knowledge areas taught in formal learning opportunities for RM consultants.

Learning Modules
• Product development process in the organization • New Requirement Management process • Team formation • Contextual inquiry techniques • Quality function deployment • Formal inspection techniques • Driving requirements in product development • Configuration management • Cost-benefit analysis

The architect chose these areas because they were well-defined and bounded by either self-paced or group-based learning opportunities. Guidelines provided in chapter 4 for creating formal learning components were followed in defining these formal learning opportunities.

The architecture included two opportunities for sharing information and experience:

◆ Biweekly meetings. Every two weeks, all RM consultants were to meet for an afternoon. These meetings were intended to provide an opportunity for consultants to share their experiences, exchange information, ask questions, and network with each other. Four expert RM consultants facilitated these meetings by helping their colleagues to reflect on their experiences and abstract lessons that could be transferred to other situations. They encouraged participants to update others on their projects, discuss potential problems, and seek advice.

◆ Notes conference. A computer-based notes conference was set up to enable RM consultants to exchange information, share experiences, post questions, seek advice, and learn from each other. Four expert RM consultants moderated the notes conference and actively participated in sharing information and experience.

The architecture did not dictate the content and agenda for the meetings and the notes conference. It simply defined the goals and the infrastructure needed for them to take place.

The development options paired each newly hired RM consultant with one of the four expert RM consultants. The role of the expert was to help the newly hired consultants

◆ become socialized to the organization by developing an understanding of the organizational climate, common practices, the product development environment, and the new RM process.

◆ assess the new consultants' RM process facilitation skills, define skill development needs, identify appropriate learning and development options, and organize the alternatives into a cohesive skill development plan.

◆ develop and fine-tune the new consultants' RM consulting skills through cognitive apprenticeship techniques.

4. Describe the interrelationships among components. The architect attempted to orchestrate components of the learning environment (shown in figure 10.2) in a complementary manner.

Figure 10.2: Components of an effective learning environment for Requirement Management consultants.

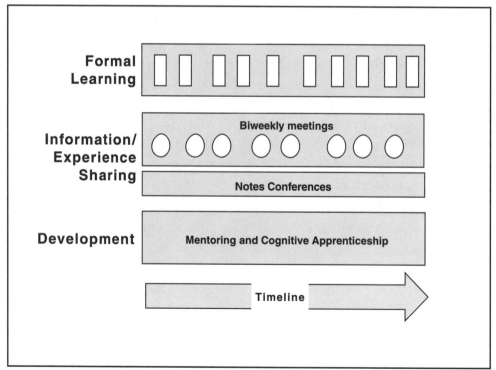

The following scenario shows how the components complement each other to help a consultant develop skills in implementing the Quality Function Deployment (QFD) technique. (QFD helps the product development team define and prioritize requirements for a new product.)

The newly hired RM consultant participates in the following sequence of learning activities:

◆ attends a one-day QFD course with fellow RM consultants to gain an overview of QFD techniques and to gain some skills in using the technique and associated tools (formal learning)

◆ participates in the implementation of the QFD technique by a new product development project team as an observer or co-facilitator. The expert RM consultant, who is skilled in implementing QFD, has primary responsibility for applying QFD in this situation. He or she provides hints to the new RM consultant during the session (cognitive apprenticeship)

◆ meets with the expert RM consultant to reflect on the experience of implementing QFD, to ask questions, and to gain greater understanding of the nuances of implementing the technique (cognitive apprenticeship)

◆ shares his experiences with his fellow RM consultants during biweekly meetings. He hears about other consultants' experiences in implementing QFD, asks questions, and fine-tunes his understanding (information sharing)

◆ asks the expert RM consultant to observe him and co-facilitate as he uses the QFD technique with his new product development project team. The expert consultant takes advantage of this opportunity to provide feedback to fine-tune the new consultant's QFD implementation skills (cognitive apprenticeship).

This scenario is only one of many possible ways in which the learners can gain and fine-tune their skills in an effective learning environment. The interrelationships of the components of the environment can reinforce each other to meet the unique needs of an individual learner.

Summary

Defining the architecture of an effective learning environment is an essential link between gathering information about the requirements and constructing the environment. One might be tempted to skip from identifying a learner's need to selecting a specific course of training to fill that need. Such an attempt, though well intentioned, can miss the mark. Defining the architecture helps to ensure that the learning solution is appropriate, that it is well designed, that it is related to the work environment, and that the organization is providing the necessary infrastructure, resources, and reward system to make it work. Guidelines developed during this phase help to maintain the architecture and to ensure that it will be updated as needed. Table 10.9 provides a checklist to guide architecture definition activities.

Table 10.9: Checklist to guide architecture definition activities.

Activity Clusters	(✓)	Actions
Analyze the requirements for the environment	❏	Strive to develop a profound understanding of business objectives, strategies, issues, and controlling factors
	❏	Analyze the tasks performed by employees and define the skills and knowledge needed to perform the tasks
	❏	Strive to understand the work environment
Decide on most appropriate learning opportunities	❏	Review skill development needs
	❏	Review attributes of learning opportunities (that is, formal learning, information sharing, development)
	❏	Match skill development needs with attributes of learning opportunities
	❏	Select and prioritize learning opportunities
Define components of the environment		**For formal learning opportunities:**
	❏	Define learning objectives
	❏	Determine scope and sequence of content
	❏	Propose alternative media and method
		For experience and information sharing:
	❏	Provide detailed descriptions of selected options (such as event driven and continuous; see chapter 4 for more detail)
	❏	Define the requirements for successful implementation of experience sharing
		For development opportunities:
	❏	Provide detailed descriptions for selected option (that is, mentoring, cognitive apprenticeships, internships)
	❏	Define processes for implementing development options (see chapters 6, 7, and 8 for more detail)
Describe interrelationships among components	❏	Define interdependencies among components
	❏	Map how learning opportunities complement each other
Identify infrastructure and resources for successful implementation	❏	Define needed infrastructure (for example, processes, practices, tools) for different components
	❏	Take advantage of existing infrastructure
	❏	Define needed resources (for example, time and budget)
Develop guidelines for implementation		**Develop guidelines in the following areas:**
	❏	identifying skill development needs
	❏	selecting learning options
	❏	organizing options into a learning and development plan
	❏	obtaining approval and allocating resources

11

Constructing the Effective Learning Environment

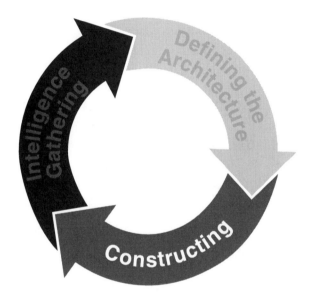

Figure 11.1: Process for creating an effective learning environment.

Chapter 10 described the process for defining the architecture of a learning environment. This chapter describes the process of implementing that architecture. This effort includes

- building the necessary infrastructure
- selecting, obtaining, customizing, and developing learning components of the environment
- selecting a subset of learning options and integrating and orchestrating the components into a total environment.

The architecture provides the blueprint for constructing the environment. Most decisions made during this phase are based on the outcomes of earlier activities (that is, intelligence gathering and defining the architecture), but many decisions make it necessary to revisit earlier decisions. The process of creating an effective learning environment is circular rather than linear. The activities involved in gathering intelligence, defining the architecture, and constructing the environment all flow into, complement, and influence one another.

The architecture does not recommend individual options for formal learning, information sharing, and development. The architecture provides placeholders into which program implementers plug individual items, as they become available. They acquire and develop individual options based on the best available alternatives.

Building the Necessary Infrastructure

The term *infrastructure* refers to the tools, processes, practices, and resources needed to implement an effective learning environment. Different infrastructure elements are required for implementation of the three components:

- formal learning (both self-paced and group-based)
- information and experience sharing
- development opportunities.

Infrastructure for self-paced learning

Self-paced formal learning consists of self-contained learning modules that learners can use and access at a convenient time and place. The infrastructure allows these modules to be obtained, stored, cataloged, and made available as a self-paced learning opportunity. For example, the medical equipment manufacturer cited earlier makes hundreds of self-paced learning modules and information units (called "learning and information bites") available to its employees through an Internet-based storage and distribution system called the Learning Network. There learners can search, browse, and download courses, documents, and related information at their desktops. Although the Internet provides an effective and convenient infrastructure for storage and distribution of self-paced learning modules, an effective and efficient infrastructure is not necessarily Internet based. Organizations that have not made a major investment in the Internet or an intranet can use a well-maintained conventional storage and distribution approach.

A robust infrastructure is a crucial success factor for implementing self-paced learning modules. Table 11.1 summarizes the attributes of such an infrastructure.

Table 11.1: Attributes of a robust infrastructure.

An infrastructure should
• Enable the organization to store, catalog, and make available learning and information modules. • Enable learners to access learning opportunities, evaluate their appropriateness, and obtain them in a timely fashion. • Enable learners to access both internal and external learning and information opportunities that meet their skill development needs. • Enable the organization to update learning opportunities continuously as new and more effective opportunities come along. • Be easy to maintain by the organization. • Be easy to use by learners. • Be capable of keeping learners' profiles and notifying them as appropriate self-paced learning opportunities become available.

Infrastructure for group-based learning

Group-based learning opportunities require collaboration, teamwork, and communication among learners and subject matter experts. Successful implementation of this type of learning opportunity requires unique infrastructure considerations, especially when the learning activities do not take place at the same time and in the same place. This infrastructure should

- provide learners with an opportunity to communicate and collaborate with each other and with subject matter experts. Both synchronized options (such as audio- and video-conferencing and online chat) and asynchronized options (such as notes conferences and electronic mail) are available.

- provide learners and facilitators with access to sources of learning material and guidelines on how to organize and implement the learning events. (This feature is similar to the infrastructure needed for accessing and obtaining self-paced learning modules.)
- provide collaborative tools that enable joint problem solving and cooperation among the learners.

Infrastructure for information and experience sharing

Information- and experience-sharing opportunities place unique requirements on an infrastructure. Depending on the size of the organization or work group, a variety of infrastructure issues may need to be addressed. For example, a notes conference, electronic forum, or mailing and messaging system allows for a continuous sharing of information in a synchronized manner. For event-driven information and experience sharing, such as forums and meetings, traditional infrastructure elements such as event scheduling and management and conference calls are available, as well as more contemporary infrastructure elements, such as intranet- and Internet-facilitated communication tools.

Infrastructure for development opportunities

Three types of development opportunities exist in the learning environment—mentoring, cognitive apprenticeships, and internships. To implement these types of learning opportunities successfully, different types of infrastructures are needed. For mentoring and cognitive apprenticeships, a process and a set of tools and guidelines should

- identify a group of qualified mentors and experts to build a mentor or expert pool
- match learners' skill development needs with available mentors or experts
- develop and implement a mentoring or cognitive apprenticeship contract between the learner and the mentor or expert
- obtain and allocate the needed resources (including time).

The following infrastructure will support the successful implementation of an internship:

- a process for identifying host organizations, enlisting them, and negotiating internship agreements with them

- a process for selecting internship candidates and assigning them to the host organizations

- processes to communicate, orient, and help learners to be fully engaged during their internship experience

- a set of tools to capture the interns' new knowledge and make it available to their colleagues in the organization.

Integrating Infrastructure Elements

The infrastructure elements must work together to meet learners' needs. For example, a review of the architecture defined for an effective learning environment for Requirements Management consultants (described in a previous chapter) showed that the following infrastructure elements were needed:

- a process for obtaining, customizing, and developing formal learning modules

- a process for storing, distributing, and scheduling the delivery of learning modules

- a process for setting up and managing the bimonthly experience- and information-sharing sessions

- a notes conference for continuously sharing what was learned, asking questions, and obtaining needed information

- processes for pairing each newly hired consultant with a mentor, defining the mentoring engagement, preparing a mentoring agreement, implementing the mentoring contract, and terminating the mentoring engagement.

An effective learning environment is a subsystem within the larger system of a work environment. Infrastructure elements must not only be integrated with each other, but must also fit harmoniously in the larger environment in order to add value. Identifying what infrastructure elements are required to implement the effective learning environment is not enough. The architect of the learning environment must also

- gain an understanding of the existing infrastructure in the organization and analyze how it can be used to fulfill the infrastructure requirements for the effective learning environment
- conduct a gap analysis between the available infrastructure and the required infrastructure to define additional investments that the organization must make.

It is highly recommended that the learning environment use the existing infrastructure as much as possible. Architects of effective learning environments should pay close attention to the work environment to ensure that tools, processes, and practices required for implementing the learning environment do not create an imbalance in the work environment. Such an imbalance can cause implementation of the learning environment to fail.

In the example of the learning environment for Requirements Management consultants, the results of the work environment analysis showed that the learning environment could use the following existing infrastructure elements:

- The existing procurement and course design processes in the Engineering Technical Training organization could be used to obtain, customize, and develop the formal learning modules.
- The existing Engineering Technical Training registration and course delivery processes could be used for storing and distributing or scheduling the delivery of learning modules.
- Weekly staff meetings, which usually lasted about two hours and did not always have a full agenda, could be devoted to information and experience sharing on the second and fourth week of each month, with the existing process used for scheduling and managing the meetings. A new set of norms was defined for these meetings to differentiate them from regular staff meetings and make them more conducive to information and experience sharing.
- A computer-based notes conference, which was already successfully used by employees for a variety of purposes, could be adopted as a means for continuously sharing experiences, asking questions, and obtaining needed information.

A formal mentoring process was the only infrastructure element that did not exist in the organization. The instructional designer had to define and institutionalize a mentoring process and a set of tools and practices.

Implementing the Architecture

Once the architect of the learning environment has defined the requirements for the infrastructure and analyzed the existing infrastructure, the organization can adopt individual elements of the required infrastructure. In the Requirement Management consulting example, the following activities took place:

- The Engineering Technical Training group agreed to use its procurement, registration, delivery processes, and course development consulting services to acquire, customize, and store the learning modules. Furthermore, they agreed to register newly hired consultants and deliver the group-based courses. They also agreed to mail self-paced instructional modules to learners on demand.

- Biweekly meetings for sharing information and experience were scheduled for mentors and Requirement Management consultants. The responsibility for building the agenda and facilitating the meetings rotated among the mentors. Norms and procedures for conducting the meetings were defined and implemented.

- A notes conference was set up as part of the organization's notes conferences system. The mentors moderated the notes conferences on a rotating basis.

- A detailed mentoring process guide, including a mentoring contract, evaluation forms, and mentor orientation learning materials, was developed for use in the mentoring process.

The process of selecting learning components and integrating them into an effective learning environment takes place at two levels: global and local.

Global implementation

Global implementation consists of activities aimed at populating the environment with learning, information, and development options. These options provide individuals and work groups within the organization with a universe of possible learning and development options from which to choose, based on their evolving needs. Based on their unique development needs, learners and work groups at a local level choose a subset of those options to construct the local version of the effective learning environment.

The term *global* indicates a macro-level implementation. Global implementation of the learning environment is the process of acquiring and developing options for formal learning, information sharing, and development, to help an organization develop the skills needed to accomplish its business objectives. These options are available to all employees and work groups regardless of their unique learning and development needs.

This process comprises the following eight clusters of tasks. The process is not linear; these tasks are performed in an iterative manner.

1. Review the description and requirements for learning options outlined in the architecture.

2. Scan possible internal and external sources to locate available options for formal learning, development, and information sharing. Depending on the types of options desired, scan different sources of information. For example, internal course catalogs, local colleges and universities, professional associations, and specialized training vendors provide possible alternatives for formal learning. For information- and experience-sharing and development options, best practices (both internal and external to the organization) are possible sources. Obtaining information on the usefulness and acceptability of these alternatives in the organization is important. An organization's past negative or positive experiences with a learning option has a direct impact on the acceptability of that option.

3. From the pool of possible alternatives for each learning option, obtain a detailed description of the material, cost, and implementation requirements. You may need to obtain examination copies or interview a vendor to obtain more detailed information.

4. Categorize and prioritize the alternatives. Alternatives fall into two categories: those that can be used "as is" or with minimal alteration, and those that need more substantial revision and

customization. Both categories are preferable to building an option from scratch. A course that takes months to build may become obsolete before it can be used.

5. Acquire the learning options, following appropriate procurement procedures in the organization. Negotiate with vendors to customize their learning and information solutions to fit the requirements outlined in the architecture.

6. Design and develop the options that are not available commercially, following the guidelines provided elsewhere in this book, and be sure to use rapid prototyping techniques.

7. Make the options accessible to the learners using the available infrastructure or create the needed infrastructure. Guidelines for creating an appropriate infrastructure are described earlier in this chapter.

8. Develop clear guidelines on how to obtain and use the options. These guidelines should enable individual learners and work groups to select, access, and utilize all options.

The global implementation of the effective learning environment for Requirement Management consultants focused on three areas: formal learning, information and experience sharing, and mentoring.

- Formal learning: Program implementers acquired, customized, or developed ten formal learning modules. They created only three modules from scratch. They selected and customized the remaining seven modules from a wide range of internal and external courses. An instructional designer and one Requirement Management process consultant worked closely with the vendors to customize the courses. They used the existing registration and delivery infrastructure for these group-based learning modules. The courses were available to the newly hired consultants and other engineers through the existing Engineer Technical Training organization.

- Experience and information sharing: The two information- and experience-sharing components were biweekly meetings and a notes conference. Implementers selected and invited meeting leaders and facilitators to build the agenda and run the meetings. A computer-based notes conference was set up using the organization's network. Implementers identified moderators for the notes conferences and then defined rules of engagement.

- Mentoring: Implementers developed a process for selecting a mentor and matching a mentor with newly hired consultants and defined a mentoring agreement. They also developed a template for the mentoring agreement.

Local implementation

The term *local* indicates a micro-level implementation: at the workgroup or individual level. Local implementation consists of the activities that select, integrate, and implement a subset of the learning options made available through global implementation. For example, in the Requirement Management consultants learning environment, nine learning modules were available. Newly hired Requirement Management consultants were encouraged to work with their mentors to assess their skill development needs and then to select and use a subset of those nine learning modules.

Guidelines for constructing an effective learning environment at the local level fall into the following five clusters of activities.

Define needed capability. Using the techniques of intelligence gathering and the skill and knowledge requirements identified while defining the architecture, the work group should identify a collection of the skills and knowledge needed to complete their work. The identified skills then guide the construction of the learning environment at the local level.

Assess skills. Once the work group has identified the needed skills at the group level, appropriate skill assessment tools and techniques, such as self-assessment, tests, peer review and observation, performance review, and customer feedback, should be used to determine the skill development needs of the individuals within the work group. After assessing individual skill development needs, the work group should aggregate the individual needs and prepare a prioritized list of group skill development needs. Facilitated group discussions and infinite diagramming techniques are possible means for creating such a list.

Select learning options. A review of available learning options made available at a global level allows them to be matched with the skill development needs of work groups and individuals. Program implementers can then select the most appropriate options for formal learning, development, and information sharing.

Planning. Implementers organize the selected learning options into Learning and Development (L&D) plans. They develop both work-group and individual plans.

- Work group L&D plan. The group plan addresses the prioritized skill development needs shared by all members of the work group. It includes a master schedule for group-based formal learning and opportunities for information sharing. For example, it outlines courses, seminars, and forums that all work-group members attend. It also includes sources of continuous information and opportunities for experience sharing (including notes conferences, prepackaged information sets, and the like) in which the whole group participates. The plan also includes needed resources (for example, time, budget, labor, facility, and infrastructure) for implementing the learning options.
- Individual L&D plan. The individual plan contains a subset of learning options from the work-group plan with additional personalized learning options for the individual. Individual plans include the following categories of information:
  - ◆ skill development needs of the individual
  - ◆ group-based formal learning and information-sharing sessions, including dates and duration
  - ◆ self-paced learning opportunities
  - ◆ mentoring and cognitive apprenticeship engagements
  - ◆ internship opportunities (including attributes of the hosting organization and duration)
  - ◆ needed resources to implement the plan

Implementing. These activities make group and individual L&D plans a reality. For example, group-based learning and information-sharing events are scheduled and delivered at the group level. The infrastructure, tools, and needed resources for implementing development options (that is, mentoring, cognitive apprenticeships, and internships) are allocated and constructed. At the individual level, self-paced learning options are acquired and utilized. Mentoring, cognitive apprenticeships, and internship engagements are finalized, agreements are negotiated and defined, and engagements are implemented and evaluated.

Summary

Creating the required infrastructure is an important step in implementing an effective learning environment. Using the current infrastructure as much as possible while investing in modifying and building a new infrastructure can be a crucial success factor. New infrastructure elements must fit harmoniously into the existing work environment. The learning components of the environment are implemented at two levels. At a global level, learning options are identified, acquired, customized, and developed in order to populate the architecture. Program implementers make the universe of potential learning options available to learners, so that they can choose appropriate options for their unique skill development needs. At a local level, the best available alternatives are selected to build a coherent, well-orchestrated learning environment for individuals and work groups. Local and global implementation are two sides of the same coin. The activities must be performed in a coordinated manner. Table 11.2 provides a checklist of the activities involved in constructing a learning environment.

Table 11.2: A checklist for learning environment construction activities.

Activity Cluster	(✓) Action
Building the infrastructure	❑ Identify infrastructure needed for various learning opportunities—formal learning, development, and information and experience sharing ❑ Gain an understanding of the existing infrastructure in the organization ❑ Analyze how the existing infrastructure can satisfy the requirement ❑ Conduct a gap analysis between available and required infrastructure ❑ Determine additional investment needed for infrastructure ❑ Establish appropriate alliances with different organizations and departments to use and build the needed infrastructure
Global implementation of the architecture	❑ Review the description and requirements for learning options outlined in the architecture ❑ Scan possible internal and external sources to locate available learning options ❑ From the pool of possible alternatives for each learning option, obtain a detailed description of the material, cost, and implementation requirements ❑ Categorize and prioritize the alternatives ❑ Acquire the learning options ❑ Design and develop the options that are not available commercially ❑ Make the options accessible to the learners ❑ Develop clear guidelines on how to obtain and use the options
Local implementation of the architecture	❑ Define the needed skills to complete the work at work-group level ❑ Determine the skill development needs of the individuals within the work group ❑ Review available learning options and match them with the skill development needs of work groups and individuals ❑ Develop a work-group plan to address the prioritized skill development needs of the group ❑ Develop individual L&D plans for work-group members ❑ Implement group and individual L&D plans

Part 4
Making Effective Learning
Environments Happen

Just as the construction of a building can be hampered by shortages of materials, changing weather conditions, and a client's changing his or her mind, the creation of an effective learning environment may involve resolving issues and overcoming obstacles.

Chapter 12 describes a number of implementation issues and obstacles that can make the creation of an effective learning environment difficult and suggests ways to resolve the issues and overcome the obstacles.

Chapter 13 explains the significance of collaboration among various functions and parts of the organization in the process of creating an effective learning environment. It also describes strategies for identifying and establishing appropriate alliances for successful implementation.

Chapter 14 looks into the future of workplace learning and considers how well an effective learning environment can equip an organization to meet its evolving skill development challenge.

Issues and Obstacles

The implementation of an effective learning environment is an organizational intervention aimed at solving the skill development challenge organizations face. As in other organizational innovations, successful implementation of a learning environment requires changes in the work environment and in other systems within the organization. The implementation of those changes is almost always associated with a number of issues and obstacles. Resolving these issues in a systemic way can allow implementation to continue.

This chapter describes a number of requirements for successful implementation of effective learning environments. Related issues and recommendations for resolving these issues are also discussed, where appropriate. Table 12.1 shows a list of requirements, a summary of issues commonly associated with these requirements, and recommended solutions.

Requirements and Recommended Solutions

The requirements listed in table 12.1 are discussed here, with each requirement followed by the recommended solutions.

Requirement: Integration of learning opportunities with work

An effective learning environment is a multifaceted, holistic learning and development system. Unlike conventional training events, which are delivered in a classroom setting, a learning environment needs to be thoroughly integrated with work. Cognitive apprenticeships and internships

Table 12.1: Requirements for successful implementation of an effective learning environment.

Requirements	Issues	Recommended Solutions
Integration of learning opportunities with work	• Disruption of work • Reduced productivity • Increased cost	• Articulate the added value of an effective learning environment • Plan actions • Allocate resources
New roles for stakeholders	• Departure from comfortable traditional roles • Lack of skill set and enthusiasm to perform new roles	• Articulate the added value • Change hiring, training, and promotion practices
Commitment from all levels	• Lack of commitment • Lack of collaboration among groups and functions within the organization	• Build a business case for an effective learning environment • Adopt a new reward system
Infrastructure	• Competing interests and priorities	• Articulate the added value • Reuse existing infrastructure • Invest in new infrastructure
Continuous improvement	• Continuous investment	• Articulate the added value of an environment
Cultural shift toward openness and sharing	• Competitive or closed culture	• Make systemic change to the organization

actually take place on the job, because actual work experiences serve modeling, reflection, and feedback purposes.

This integration of work and learning activities is a major change for some organizations. Stakeholders in organizations—managers, employees, or customers—may perceive the attempt to integrate learning activities with work as a disruption to the work. If not managed effectively, the integration of learning activities with work can have a negative impact on the work of the organization. Failure to deal effectively with this issue can compromise the integrity of the learning environment and lead to the creation of an artificial learning situation.

Recommended solutions.

- Emphasize the benefits. Position the integration aspect of the learning environment carefully with all stakeholders. Help them to understand that the complexity and dynamic nature of the required skills make them difficult to teach in isolated, artificial, make-believe learning activities. Help managers, employees, and customers realize that an effective learning environment is a business necessity, not a luxury. Explain the benefits of an effective learning environment to all stakeholders, so that they do not see learning as an intrusion in the workplace, and so that they make the necessary accommodations.

- Help line managers articulate any potential negative impact of this integration on the work environment. Support line managers so that they can engage stakeholders in developing plans to reduce potential negative impacts.

- Define the resources needed to implement appropriate changes successfully. Time is usually the most important resource. Experienced colleagues need time to communicate with learners, to model desirable behaviors, to have learners perform work under their observation, to provide feedback to learners, and to help learners reflect on their experiences and generalize from their learning. Learning activities may require adjustment in the workflow.

Requirement: New roles for stakeholders

Implementation of an effective learning environment requires changes in the traditional roles performed by members of the training department, by line and business managers, and by the learners themselves. In conventional training settings, roles and expectations are relatively well defined. Training consultants, in cooperation with subject matter experts, define, design, and develop training solutions. Instructors usually deliver training solutions that involve classroom presentation. Some instructors are subject matter experts from line organizations. They teach courses based on a predefined schedule and with a well-defined time commitment. For the most part, the involvement of line and business managers in making training events happen is very limited. They allocate funds and delegate most of their responsibilities to the training function.

Successful creation and implementation of an effective learning environment requires a significant change in the roles of the training department and line and business managers. The following list examines the different roles that members of the organization must play in different phases of the implementation of an effective learning environment:

- Defining the architecture of the environment. This role involves defining what is required by the business, the work environment, and the learners. It also involves defining, designing, and orchestrating components of the learning environment and defining requirements for its successful implementation.

- Constructing the environment. This role involves procurement, customization, and development of formal learning components. It also involves planning mentoring, cognitive apprenticeship, and internship opportunities.

- Building the necessary infrastructure. This role involves defining the necessary infrastructure and developing the tools, processes, and practices needed for implementing the environment.

- Mentoring and providing cognitive apprenticeships. This role involves sharing expertise and experiences with colleagues and helping them to develop needed skills.

- Hosting internships. This role involves accepting learners and providing them with a hospitable learning environment to gain needed skills.

- Constructing an effective learning environment at a local level. This role involves making formal learning opportunities accessible to work groups, making the necessary adjustments to the work environment, allocating resources, and adjusting the reward structure to encourage employees to support and participate actively in the learning environment.

The roles listed above clearly demonstrate a significant expansion of the training department's traditional roles in developing and managing the delivery of courses and training events. It also shows more active involvement and participation of the business and line management—a departure from their traditional role of allocating funds and delegating responsibilities to the training department. These changes in roles and responsibilities, like any other changes, are not easy. New skill sets, processes, and tools are needed to make these changes happen. Failure to recognize the new roles and actively lead the change can be detrimental to the successful implementation of an effective learning environment.

Recommended solutions.

- Articulate the added value of an effective learning environment. The creation of an effective learning environment is a business necessity, not a luxury. Conventional skill development methods are no longer sufficient to meet the skill development needs of organizations. Advocates of effective learning environments need to explain this new reality to stakeholders, encouraging them to accept new roles and strive toward helping the organization meet its skill development challenges.

- Help people acquire the skills, knowledge, and commitment to play new roles. It is imperative to align hiring, development, and promotion practices with training department practices to ensure that employees are willing and able to make effective learning environments happen. Line and business managers also should ensure that employees and managers are committed to the skill development of their colleagues and that they have the right skills to perform these new roles. For example, there is a need to help experienced employees and experts develop skills in mentoring and cognitive apprenticeship.

Requirement: Commitment from all levels

Unlike conventional training interventions, which the training department mainly defines, manages, and implements, implementation of an effective learning environment needs a significant commitment from a number of people at different levels of the organization. Table 12.2 shows tasks that a variety of stakeholders should perform to make an effective learning environment happen.

To make an effective learning environment happen, many people from different functions within the organization need to collaborate and perform new, unconventional tasks. This collaboration is a challenge, especially in large and fragmented organizations. Lack of needed commitment is a significant barrier in implementing effective learning environments.

Table 12.2: Tasks performed by various stakeholders.

Stakeholders	Tasks
Line manager	• Allocate needed resources • Encourage experts and experienced people to mentor and conduct cognitive apprenticeships • Work with colleagues inside and outside the organization to identify internship opportunities • Help employees identify their skill development needs and select, customize, and utilize learning and development opportunities • Implement a new reward system to drive the right behaviors in support of the learning environment
Business managers	Invest in the following areas: • Build an infrastructure for the learning environment • Acquire and develop learning opportunities • Acquire needed resources • Build a reward structure that drives the right behavior
Employees	• Play an active role in defining their skill development needs • Actively seek opportunities for developing the needed skills
Training professionals	• Redefine roles • Actively work toward defining, constructing, coordinating, evaluating, and continuously improving the learning environments
Experienced and knowledgeable employees	Share their knowledge with their colleagues through • participating in information and experience sharing • mentoring and providing cognitive apprenticeships to their colleagues

Recommended solutions.

- Articulating the added value of an effective learning environment and communicating business imperatives to all stakeholders.

- Adopting an appropriate reward system that encourages commitment to successful implementation of an effective learning environment by rewarding experienced employees and experts for sharing their expertise by either mentoring their colleagues or providing cognitive apprenticeships. The reward system should encourage employees to take an active role in defining their skill development needs and fulfilling those needs and to collaborate with other departments to make the effective learning environment happen. It should encourage line and business managers to make necessary accommodations to the work environment and allocate the needed resources.

Requirement: Infrastructure

Successful implementation of a learning environment requires an infrastructure—the tools, processes, practices, and resources needed to implement the environment. Creation of a robust infrastructure requires a major investment by the organization. The competing priorities of an organization may make allocation of needed resources difficult.

Recommended solutions.

- Articulate the added value of an effective learning environment. Building a business case for investment in infrastructure is crucial.
- Reuse the availe infrastructure. Use the existing infrastructure as much as possible to reduce the need for a major investment in the early stages of creating the environment. The procedures for analyzing infrastructure needs and available resources are useful for identifying elements that can be used in the short run with minimal investment.
- Make new investment in the infrastructure. Once the learning environment is established, a business case should be made for making new and continuous investment in the infrastructure. A robust infrastructure makes implementation of a learning environment more efficient.

Requirement: Continuous improvement

Effective learning environments are not static. The dynamic nature of an organization's skill development needs requires the constant updating of an effective learning environment:

- Frequently update the formal learning components of an environment
- Continuously add new internship sites
- Continuously expand the pool of mentors and experts for cognitive apprenticeships.

Continuous improvement of a learning environment requires a long investment period. Organizations that are accustomed to creating a training budget on a quarterly basis may not be receptive to long-term and continuous investment in the creation and maintenance of an effective learning environment.

Recommended solutions. Articulate the added value of an effective learning environment. To demonstrate the need for continuous investment, make a business case for continuous and long-term investment in the learning environment. Advocates of the effective learning environment should help line and business managers understand that the creation of a sound mentoring program with the needed infrastructure cannot happen overnight. The need for a longer investment period coexists with a need for agility in developing skills and fighting skill obsolescence. Rapid prototyping techniques can enable an organization to use its current infrastructure to make the learning and development solutions available. In a parallel track, however, the organization should continuously invest in the necessary infrastructure to enable continuous improvement of the learning environment.

Requirement: Cultural shift toward openness and sharing

Successful implementation of an effective learning environment requires a new set of norms. Only an organizational culture that encourages openness and sharing of information can successfully implement the information- and experience-sharing component of the environment. The mentoring and cognitive apprenticeship component of the environment also requires that experienced employees and experts be willing to share their knowledge and expertise with their colleagues and help them actively and effectively with their development.

An organization that is not open, in which employees are reluctant to share their knowledge, is not conducive to implementing an effective learning environment. Openness and a willingness to share information are cultural attributes of an organization. They are a product of its history, current expectations and practices, and reward system. Changing the culture of an organization requires a major commitment at all levels and a systemic approach. Management involvement is crucial.

Recommended solutions.

- Make information and experience sharing an integral component of every employee's job. Use appropriate metrics to measure the right behavior.
- Establish a reward system to encourage the right behaviors.
- Provide appropriate behavioral models at all levels of the organization to encourage openness.

Summary

This chapter discusses a number of requirements for successful implementation of effective learning environments. Advocates of effective learning environments should realize that they need to adopt a systemic approach and a multifaceted strategy to make effective learning environments happen. A number of recommendations made in this chapter can resolve implementation issues.

The implementation of an effective leaning environment is a major change in an organization. It involves new roles, changes in investment strategies, and sometimes a major change in an organization's culture. These changes affect existing work activities profoundly. They are part of a continuous improvement effort. Such changes require commitment from all levels of the organization. The most important factor in obtaining that commitment is an understanding of the learning environment itself: its benefits to different members of the organization, its importance to the continued success of the organization, and its investment value.

13

Establishing Alliances

Implementation of an effective learning environment requires a cultural change in an organization. Part of that change is that different parts of an organization must learn to work together more closely.

Many of the activities involved in the creation of an effective learning environment are either new or are performed in a new context. Many require sponsorship, support, and cooperation of people from different groups and functions. Establishing alliances within an organization is very important in making the learning environment a reality.

The creation of an effective learning environment, like other organizational interventions, requires a champion. The champion articulates the added value of the environment, gains sponsorship and support to obtain needed resources, and forges appropriate alliances and partnerships to make the environment happen.

This chapter describes the champion's role in forging necessary alliances and examines major categories of tasks performed during the creation of an effective learning environment to identify needed alliances.

Roles of a Champion

The champion's role is extremely important in initiating and institutionalizing a learning environment. The champion can come from line or business management or from a function (for example, learning and development or human resources). A champion is both leader and advocate. The champion must

- recognize the business imperatives for creating an effective learning environment
- articulate the added value of an effective learning environment
- identify major stakeholders and define needs and expectations for each stakeholder
- communicate the significance of the environment to stakeholders and gain their support
- obtain resources to build the needed infrastructure and to implement the environment.

Required Activities

Once an organization recognizes the need for an effective learning environment, the champion begins the work of articulating its added value and identifying and enlisting sponsors and colleagues who can make it happen. The following is a partial list of the alliances that he or she should establish:

- Business management. Business managers are ultimately responsible for the success of their business. They need to acquire and maintain the capabilities needed to run the business. They make investment decisions to this end and are typically very interested in the business impact of creating a learning environment. Their sponsorship is essential in obtaining the resources needed to create the learning environment.
- Line management. Line managers are interested in people development and are responsible for acquiring and maintaining the required capabilities to meet the business objectives. Their support is essential in creating an effective learning environment in their group and in making the necessary adjustments in the work environment to accommodate the learning environment.
- Technical community. Knowledgeable and experienced employees play an important role in creating an effective learning environment. Their active participation is essential in mentoring, cognitive apprenticeships, and experience- and information-sharing activities.
- Information technology (IT) community. The IT community plays an important role in creating the needed infrastructure for experi-

ence and information sharing and for the electronic storage and distribution of self-paced learning materials.

- Logistics and distribution. This function is an important component in facilitating the distribution of learning and information solutions to the learners. The champion should develop an understanding of the current distribution infrastructure and practices to use them effectively. The cooperation and support of this function are essential in implementing an effective learning environment.

- Purchasing. Learning solutions used in the formal learning component of an effective learning environment are usually obtained from external sources. The dynamic nature of skills in some professions makes it more reasonable to acquire rather than develop these learning materials. Procurement of learning and information solutions may require sophisticated negotiations with vendors on price, customization, frequency of updates, and intellectual property issues. A productive working relationship with the purchasing function of the organization can lead to effective and economical procurement of learning solutions.

- Human resources. The HR function plays an important role in creating effective learning environments. Successful implementation of an effective learning environment requires a change in the roles and behaviors of employees. For example, experienced and knowledgeable employees must share their experience-based knowledge, mentor others, and participate in cognitive apprenticeships. Learners must actively seek and pursue learning opportunities, and managers must allocate needed resources and actively endorse the learning environment. All these changes in the roles and behaviors require the establishment of new expectations and the implementation of a new reward structure. The support and cooperation of the HR community help to facilitate the necessary changes.

- Internal and external organizations that provide internship opportunities. Internships are an important part of the development component of a learning environment. Host organizations play an important role in successful implementation of internships. The champion should establish strong relationships with host organizations to enlist their support.

- Learning and development (L&D) community. The champion may come from the L&D community, but regardless of the champion's organizational affiliation, he or she should enlist the support of colleagues in this community. The L&D community should play a leadership role in making effective learning environments happen.

Alliances and Creation of an Effective Learning Environment

The alliances established within an organization can support the creation of an effective learning environment at each stage of creation.

Intelligence gathering

Intelligence-gathering activities make it possible to define the requirements for the environment, to identify existing learning and development opportunities and support infrastructure, and to collect feedback for assessing the effectiveness of the environment and its components in order to improve it continuously. Collection of valid and reliable information requires cooperation, openness, and commitment from a number of people and groups within an organization. The champion, the architect of the environment, and implementers of the learning environment need the support and willingness of knowledgeable employees and of those who possess information to collect, analyze, and validate reliable information. The champion identifies these individuals, enlists their support, and negotiates appropriate arrangements for collecting the needed information.

Defining the architecture

A learning specialist defines the architecture based on the requirements defined during the intelligence-gathering process. Once the architecture is defined, the champion communicates to those affected, obtains their support, and enlists their commitment during the construction and implementation processes. Those affected include learners, experienced and knowledgeable colleagues and subject matter experts, and those in line management, business management, learning and development, human resources, information systems, purchasing, distribution, and host organizations.

Constructing the environment

The activities in this cluster involve not only obtaining, customizing, developing, and orchestrating components of the learning environment, but also building the needed tools, processes, and practices to implement the learning environment. A number of organizations and functions, including business management, purchasing, line management, learning and development, human resources, information systems, and distribution, must collaborate.

Summary

The creation of an effective learning environment, like other organizational initiatives, requires a champion. The champion's tasks include envisioning the environment, articulating the added value of the environment, identifying sponsors, establishing alliances, obtaining needed resources, and coordinating the efforts. Establishing alliances within an organization is essential for making an effective learning environment a reality. The champion must strive to establish alliances with colleagues in a number of groups and functions. Table 13.1 lists the tasks performed by different groups and functions in making an effective learning environment happen.

Table 13.1: Activities performed by different groups in an effective learning environment.

Groups and Functions	Activities
Business management	• Sponsor the learning activities • Allocate resources to create the needed infrastructure and acquire and develop components of the environment
Line management	• Make the necessary adjustments in the work environment to accommodate the learning environment • Provide needed resources to implement learning environment • Encourage colleagues to participate in information sharing and development activities • Support and encourage employees to take advantage of learning opportunities
Information systems	• Create the needed infrastructure • Facilitate use of the current infrastructure
Logistics and distribution	• Facilitate the distribution of learning and information solutions to the learners • Participate in building a new infrastructure for distributing learning solutions
Purchasing	• Facilitate procurement of learning solutions • Negotiate with vendors on price, customization, frequency of updates, and intellectual property issues
Human resources	• Establish new expectations and implement a new reward structure to encourage employees support, commitment, and participation • Facilitate implementation of the learning environment
Technical community	• Participate in defining requirements for the learning environment • Participate in mentoring and cognitive apprenticeships • Participate in experience- and information-sharing activities
Hosting organization	• Participate in planning internship • Sponsor employees during internship • Provide a hospitable learning environment for the learners
Learning and development community	• Participate in defining the requirements for the learning environment • Participate in defining the architecture • Design and develop learning opportunities • Participate in procurement of learning opportunities • Coordinate implementation of the learning environment • Participate in assessing the effectiveness of the learning environment and its business impact

Future Role of Effective Learning Environments

The ability to learn faster than your competitors may be the only sustainable competitive advantage.

— Peter Senge (1995)

An effective learning environment is a solution to the skill development and maintenance challenge that contemporary organizations face. The challenge is a product of the cumulative effect of the following five factors: (1) complexity of the required skills to complete the work of the organization, (2) constant changes in the required skills, (3) a lack of resident expertise to help employees develop all required skills, (4) a changing workforce, which results in a loss of organizational experience and history, and (5) a lack of uniformity in skill deficiencies among employees.

An effective learning environment is a collection of learning opportunities that surrounds employees and enables them to develop new skills and continuously upgrade their existing skills. The learning opportunities in the environment include formal courses and learning modules (both self-paced and group-based), development engagements (such as internships, cognitive apprenticeships, and mentoring), and opportunities to share experience and information. Based on business needs, individual skill development needs, individual learning styles, and the constraints of the work environment, employees select and participate in a subset of the learning opportunities provided in the environment. An effective learning environment must therefore be multifaceted, continuous, rigorous, and demanding. It must be integrated with the work and responsive to the changing business needs. Finally, it must accommodate employees' skill development needs.

The methodology (that is, a process and a set of tools and guidelines) presented in this book for creating effective learning environments enables an organization to do the following:

- continuously collect and analyze information by defining requirements for the learning environment based on constantly changing business needs, an evolving work environment, and continuously changing skill development needs of the employees; and by assessing the effectiveness and business impact of the environment and using the information to improve the learning environment continuously

- define an architecture for a learning environment

- construct the environment by creating and adopting the infrastructure that is needed to implement the environment effectively and developing, acquiring, and orchestrating a set of learning opportunities to help employees develop the required skills.

The guidelines presented in this book can help an organization overcome obstacles in creating and implementing an effective learning environment. Likewise, the recommendations presented in this book can help an organization to establish appropriate alliances and partnerships that help to make an effective learning environment happen.

Effective learning environments are a strategic tool for enhancing workplace learning and performance. They help organizations achieve business objectives and meet productivity and quality metrics. The challenge of helping employees to develop new skills and fight skill obsolescence is never ending. As the 21st century begins, the complexity of the skill development challenge will almost certainly increase. The following factors are likely to increase the complexity of the evolving organizations themselves and to make the skill development challenge even more formidable:

- Customers' needs, demands, and requirements will continue to change rapidly as organizations enter a global marketplace and expand their customer base.

- Organizations' portfolios of products and services will change more rapidly to accommodate the evolving needs and expectations of a global customer base and to offset competitive pressure. Products will become more complex (that is, complete solutions will replace individual product solutions) and, as a result, product planning, selling, and servicing will become more complex.

- The tools, technologies, processes, and practices that employees use to complete the work of the organization will change continuously in the decentralized, global organizations of the future.

- Competitive pressure will increase dramatically. Increased competition will force organizations to improve their technology continuously, to invest in new product development, and to reduce cycle time.

- The nature of the relationships among organizations will change rapidly, and the complexity of those relationships will increase. A single organization will become simultaneously a competitor, a supplier, a customer, and a partner of another organization.

- The regulatory environment will change dramatically. Global organizations will have to operate according to complex regulations imposed by different host countries and at the same time adopt new ways of doing business in free trade zones to cope with deregulation.

A full discussion of future trends and their impact on the evolving organizations of the 21st century is beyond the scope of this chapter. Readers are encouraged to review Toffler (1990). A glimpse into the future is sufficient, however, to demonstrate the increased complexity of evolving organizations. The implications for the skill development challenge that organizations face are daunting.

A growing number of organizations have recognized the need for creative solutions to meet this skill development challenge. These organizations are taking significant steps to develop and preserve their intellectual capital (that is, employees' knowledge, skills, experiences, and ideas). According to Stuller (1998), an estimated 250 to 300 organizations within the United States have created senior executive positions, such as chief learning officer (CLO) or chief knowledge officer (CKO), to bring a strategic focus to their skill development and knowledge management efforts. According to another estimate (cited by Stuller, 1998), 20 percent of *Fortune* 500 companies have a CKO or CLO whose task is to "develop and deploy a corporation's brainpower."

In the evolving organizations of the future, traditional training techniques (such as classroom training events) alone will not be sufficient for developing and maintaining a complex set of ever-changing skills. The learning opportunities that these organizations provide must

- be accommodating to the needs of a diverse, decentralized, and global employee population with a variety of skill development needs, learning styles, work habits, and employment arrangements (for example, full-time, part-time, contracting).

- extend beyond the boundaries of the organization to enable employees to tap into the expertise of knowledge creators, regardless of their location and organizational affiliation.

- enable employees to gain content knowledge as well as heuristic knowledge, control strategies, and learning strategies (see chapter 7 for a more detailed description of various knowledge types).

- enable employees to access experience-based knowledge of their colleagues as the knowledge becomes available and/or as they need it.

- use both technology-based and people-based techniques for learning and sharing experience and information.

- be conducive to the development of complex skill sets. Learning experiences must allow employees to observe the complex behaviors of master performers on the job, model their behaviors while being observed, and receive meaningful feedback as they successively approximate the desired behavior.

- use multiple learning options in an organized manner to deepen employees' understanding and expand their skill set. For example, an employee might attend a course to develop basic skills, participate in a project with an experienced colleague to observe how the skills are implemented, meet with an expert to reflect on the experience and gain greater understanding of the nuances of implementing the skills, share these new insights with colleagues, and receive feedback.

- be integrated with work to provide context-based learning experiences, as opposed to artificial, make-believe learning experiences.

Learning opportunities with the above attributes are the building blocks for constructing an effective learning environment accommodating to the business needs of the organization and the learning needs of the employees. An effective learning environment constructed using the framework and methodology discussed in this book can help evolving organizations of the future to meet their skill development challenge.

Glossary

Capability. The required skills and knowledge to complete the work of the organization.

Capacity. The number of people with required skills to achieve an organization's objectives.

Cognitive apprenticeship. A learning opportunity intended to help learners develop a complex set of cognitive skills, such as decision making or problem solving, under the supervision of an expert performer.

Cognitive apprenticeship methods.
- In *modeling* the expert provides the learner with an opportunity to observe the expert carrying out a task so that the learner may develop a conceptual model of the processes required to complete the task.
- In *coaching* the expert observes the learner while he or she carries out a task and offers hints, feedback, reminders, and suggestions to bring the learner's performance closer to the expert's.
- In *scaffolding* the expert provides support to help the learner carry out a task. This support is in the form of reminders and help. The expert might carry out parts of the overall task that the learner cannot yet manage.
- In *articulation* the expert helps the learner to articulate his or her knowledge, reasoning, or problem-solving processes as he or she carries out the task.
- In *reflection* the expert helps the learner to compare his or her own problem-solving processes with the ones used by the expert. Reflection is used for self-evaluation.

- In *exploration* the expert pushes the learner into a mode of problem solving on his or her own where there is no clear approach to solving the problem.

Constructing the environment. These activities put the architecture of the learning environment into operation. Environment implementers acquire or develop specific options for formal learning, development, and information sharing and cultivate the environment.

Defining the architecture for the environment. These activities create a blueprint for the environment. Architects define and design the components of the environment and also integrate them into an architecture for a holistic, multifaceted learning environment.

Development opportunities. These opportunities represent structured on-the-job learning with well-defined outcomes, duration, and required resources. Unlike traditional training interventions that are designed for an average or typical learner, development opportunities respond to the unique needs of the learner. Three types of development opportunities exist in an effective learning environment—mentoring, cognitive apprenticeships, and internships or sabbaticals.

Formal learning. These opportunities are well bounded, with clearly defined learning outcomes. They help learners gain knowledge or develop skills in a regulated, predefined fashion. These learning opportunities can be self-paced or group based, instructor led or technology based. Examples are a computer-based learning module, an instructional video, a two-day workshop, a simulation, or a course in a local college.

Formal learning, group-based. In these learning opportunities a group of learners interact with each other and possibly with a subject matter expert, instructor, or source of information to gain the needed knowledge or to develop the desired skills. Examples of group-based learning opportunities are lectures, case studies, facilitated discussions, group simulations, workshops, and other types of team-based collaborative learning situations. Group-based learning usually uses face-to-face communication among the learners and subject matter experts, although technology-based meeting alternatives (for example, IBTV, teleconferencing, collaborative distance communication software) can reduce the need to travel to a central location.

Formal learning, self-paced. These formal learning opportunities represent independent learning situations in which learners progress through learning activities at their own pace. Examples are tutorials and text-based, video-based, and computer-based training.

Global implementation. The term *global* indicates a macro-level implementation. Global implementation of the learning environment is the process of acquiring and developing options for formal learning, information sharing, and development, to help an organization develop the needed skills to accomplish its business objectives.

Information and experience sharing. These opportunities help employees to reinforce existing skills and knowledge, to stay current with new developments that impact their work, and to revise skills and knowledge. Unlike formal learning opportunities, information and experience sharing tends to be spontaneous. These opportunities can be event driven (such as having a brown bag session on an upcoming model of a product) or continuous (such as a regularly scheduled conference call among the sales force members to exchange the latest information).

Information sharing, continuous. These opportunities are available continuously to learners who are seeking information and who want to access their colleagues' experience and knowledge. Unlike event-driven opportunities, which require a group of learners to assemble either physically or virtually during a predefined time interval, continuous information and experience-sharing opportunities can take place at any time.

Information sharing, event-driven. Opportunities in which a group of learners assemble during a predefined time period to analyze and discuss ideas, to dissect solutions, or to study trends and their implication for current practice. These events may be highly structured with a predefined agenda, such as a forum or panel discussion, or spontaneous, such as a brainstorming brown bag session.

Infrastructure. This term refers to the tools, processes, practices, and resources needed to implement an effective learning environment.

Intelligence gathering. These activities help to define the requirements for the learning environment and help to assess the effectiveness and business impact of the learning environment.

Internship. This learning opportunity helps learners develop a thorough understanding of the best practices of a host organization through immersion in another organization, which may be internal or external.

Knowledge types.

- *Domain knowledge* includes facts, concepts, and procedures associated with a given profession (for example, law, information technology service, accounting, or instructional design).

- *Heuristic knowledge* includes knowledge of effective techniques and approaches for accomplishing the tasks that might be regarded as "tricks of the trade" or "rules of thumb."

- *Control strategies* involve the management of the problem-solving process. They consist of strategies that help an expert to set goals, select the most appropriate problem-solving strategy among the various possible strategies, monitor implementation of the strategy, decide when to change strategies, and evaluate the outcome.

- *Learning strategies* include knowledge of how to learn. These strategies help people assess what they know and determine what they need to know. They also help them determine how to explore new areas of knowledge, how to get new knowledge, and how to integrate the new knowledge with what they already know. Learners who are engaged in self-directed learning use these strategies.

Lack of resident expertise. As organizations focus on their core competencies and establish new alliances and partnerships to provide complex products and services, they may find that not all expertise required to complete the work or to train employees will reside within the organization.

Lack of uniformity in skill deficiency. Learning and development needs of individual employees are unique and different. Different groups and individuals in the same group have unique skill development requirements depending on their experiences, prior knowledge, and alternative ways of processing information.

Local implementation. The term *local* indicates a micro-level implementation—one at a work group or individual level. Local implementation consists of the activities that select, integrate, and implement a subset of the learning options made available through global implementation.

Mentoring. This learning opportunity is intended to help learners become socialized to the larger context of an organization, profession, or industry. The socialization is achieved through one-on-one work with a seasoned colleague.

Rapid prototyping. Borrowed from the software engineering discipline, rapid prototyping is an iterative process of design in which the designer discovers the problem and learning solution through the use of prototypes.

Research methods. In the *qualitative research approach,* a researcher uses an emergent design and makes decisions about the data collection strategies during the study and presents the results in a narration with words. In the *quantitative research approach,* a researcher follows an established set of procedures and steps that are established before data collection and presents statistical results with numbers.

References

Brown, John S., Allen Collins, and Duguid. "Situated Cognition and the Culture of Learning." *Educational Researcher,* volume 18, number 1, 1989, 32–42.

Collins, Allen, John S. Brown, and A. Holum. "Cognitive Apprenticeship: Making Thinking Visible." *American Educator: The Professional Journal of the American Federation of Teachers,* volume 15, 1991, 6–11.

Collins, Allen, John S. Brown, and Susa E. Newman. "Cognitive Apprenticeship: Teaching the Craft of Reading, Writing, and Mathematics." In Lauren B. Resnick (editor), *Knowing, Learning, and Instruction: Essays in Honor of Robert Glaser* (453–494). Hillsdale, NJ: Lawrence Erlbaum, 1989.

Dick, Walter, and Lou Carey. *The Systematic Design of Instruction* (4th edition). Glenview, IL: Scott, Foresman, and Co., 1991.

Dills, Charles R., and Alexander J. Romiszowski. *Instructional Development Paradigms.* Englewood Cliffs, NJ: Educational Technology Publications, 1997.

Fink, Arlene, and Jacqueline B. Kosecoff. *How to Conduct Surveys: A Step-by-Step Guide.* Newbury Park, CA: Sage Publications, 1985.

Gagne, Robert M., Leslie J. Briggs, and Walter W. Wager. *Principles of Instructional Design.* Fort Worth, TX: Holt, Rinehart Winston, Inc., 1992.

Gradous, Deane (editor). *Systems Theory Applied to Human Resource Development*. Alexandria, VA: American Society for Training & Development, 1989.

Hayman, John L. Jr. "The Systems Approach and Education." *Educational Forum*, volume 38, May 1974, 493–501.

Heinich, Robert (editor), Michael Molenda, James D. Russell, and Michel Smaldino. *Instructional Media and Technologies for Learning* (5th edition). Englewood Cliffs, NJ: Prentice Hall, 1996.

Hendricks, W. (editor). *Coaching, Mentoring and Managing: Breakthrough Strategies To Solve Performance Problems and Build Winning Teams*. Franklin Lakes, NJ: Career Press, 1996.

Kirkpatrick, Donald L. *Evaluating Training Programs: The Four Levels* (2d edition). San Francisco, CA: Berrett-Koehler, 1998.

Kochan, Thomas A., and Michael Useem. *Transforming Organizations*. New York: Oxford University Press, 1992.

Kram, Kathy E. *Mentoring at Work: Developmental Relationships in Organizational Life*. Lanham, MD: University Press of America, 1988.

Lundholm, Jeanne *Mentoring: The Mentor's Perspective*. Cambridge, MA: MIT, 1982.

McMillan, James H, and Sally Schumacher. *Research in Education: A Conceptual Introduction* (3d edition). New York: HarperCollins College Publishers, 1993.

Murray, Margo. *Beyond the Myths and Magic of Mentoring: How To Facilitate an Effective Mentoring Program*. San Francisco: Jossey-Bass Publishers, 1993.

Robbins, Stephen P. *Organizational Theory: Structure, Design, and Applications* (3d edition). Englewood Cliffs, NJ: Prentice Hall, 1990.

Rosenbach, William E., and Robert L. Taylor (editors). *Contemporary Issues in Leadership* (3d edition). Boulder, CO: Westview Press, 1993.

Rossett, Allison. *Training Needs Assessment*. Englewood Cliffs, NJ: Educational Technology Publications, 1987.

Senge, Peter M. *The Fifth Discipline: The Art and Practice of the Learning Organization.* New York, NY: Bantam Doubleday Dell Publishing Group, Inc., 1990.

Shea, Gordon F. *Mentoring: Helping Employees Reach Their Full Potential.* Saranac Lake, NY: AMACOM, 1994.

Snow, Richard "Aptitude Theory: Yesterday, Today, and Tomorrow." *Educational Psychologist,* volume 27, number 1, 1992, 5–32.

Snow, Richard, and Judy Swanson. "Instructional Psychology: Aptitude, Adaptability, and Assessment." *Annual Review of Psychology,* Volume 43, 1992, 583–626.

Stuller, Jay "Chief of Corporate Smarts." *Training,* April 1998, 28–34.

Toffler, Alvin. *Powershift.* New York: Bantam, 1990.

The Author

Reza Sisakhti has been a workplace learning and performance improvement practitioner for the past two decades. His experience includes the following:

- assisting senior managers to adopt a systemic approach to human performance improvement in support of their business objectives
- developing human performance improvement models and processes
- defining competency models
- defining and designing learning and development programs
- conducting training business impact and cost-benefit analyses
- conducting business, needs, audience, job, tasks, skills, process, and organizational analyses.

Sisakhti is a senior educational consultant at Digital Equipment Corporation. He is also a lecturer at the School of Education, Boston University, where he has been teaching graduate courses in computer-based instruction and instructional design since 1986.

Sisakhti earned his Ph.D. in instructional systems technology from Indiana University in 1982, where he taught and served as an instructional design consultant prior to joining Digital Equipment Corporation in 1983. He received his Executive M.B.A. from the University of New Hampshire in 1992.